Fraud and Fallible Judgment

Fraud and Fallible Judgment

Varieties of Deception in the Social and Behavioral Sciences

EDITED BY

Nathaniel J. Pallone
James J. Hennessy

Transaction Publishers
New Brunswick (U.S.A.) and London (U.K.)

Copyright © 1995 by Transaction Publishers, New Brunswick, New Jersey 08903. The preface and chapters 3, 4, 5, 6, 8, 10, 11, and 12 originally appeared in *Society* 31:3 in 1994. Chapter 2 originally appeared in *American Scholar* 60:4 in 1991 under the title "Scientific Fraud." Chapter 7 originally appeared in *Academic Questions* 4:1 in 1990–91 under the title "On the Self-Suppression of Academic Freedom." Chapter 9 originally appeared in *Society* 30:3 in 1993.

This book is printed on acid-free paper that meets the American National Standard for Permanence of Paper for Printed Library Materials.

Library of Congress Catalog Number: 94-46395
ISBN: 1-56000-813-X
Printed in the United States of America

Library of Congress Cataloging-in-Publication Data

Fraud and fallible judgment : varieties of deception in the social and behavioral sciences / edited by Nathaniel J. Pallone and James J. Hennessy.

   p. cm.
Includes bibliographical references (p.   ) and index.
ISBN 1-56000-813-X (pbk.: alk. paper)
   1. Social sciences—Research—Moral and ethical aspects. 2. Social scientists—Professional ethics. 3. Fraud in science. I. Pallone, Nathaniel J. II. Hennessy, James.
H62.F698   1995
305.9'309—dc20   94-46395
                                                     CIP

Contents

Part III: Attribution and Misattribution of Deception

Preface

In the wonderful short story "When Greek Meets Greek"—concerning a mutual scam between donors and recipients of degrees at the non-existent "St. Ambrose College of Oxford"—Graham Greene, the most flinty of English writers, allows himself a conclusion of his own. "There were bigger frauds all round them; officials of the Ministries passed carrying little portfolios; controllers of this and that purred by in motor-cars, and men with the big blank faces of advertisement hoardings strode purposefully in khaki with scarlet tabs down Park Lane from the Dorchester. Their fraud was a small one by the world's standard? and a harmless one: the boy from Borstal and the girl from nowhere at all."

One can imagine that readers would react similarly to this issue of fraud in the social sciences. After all, when compared to the implications of cancer research or solutions to age-old mathematical puzzles, the problems posed by social science research pale in significance. Still, even there, especially when the issues dwelled upon are intelligence quotients and tests, risks of drug use to the urban population, or racial differentials in criminal behavior, the policy consequences are sufficiently weighty to cause a worldly concern about fraudulence. In essence, it is less a matter of fraud than of the nature of truth in social relations and experiential rules. Dealing with epistemology as a problem of social science permits the absorption of philosophy in small doses—but at this point, any dose will do.

The issue of fraud—as several contributors make quite clear—moves far beyond a simple dictionary definition of duplicity. The social sciences hardly provide an area where painting spots on mice to prove an oncological point can be replicated. Rather, social scientists are faced with a full range of options—from plagiarizing of data and ideas to quiet suppression of information that might cause harm or injury to a group the researcher feels has already been sufficiently harmed or injured in the past. Whatever its nature, the word "fraud" itself carries a terrible sting. Allegations of this sort can be used—and in the case of the British psychologist Cyril Burt were used—to destroy careers and control "dangerous" thoughts.

Fraud is also of concern to the internal life of a discipline—raising issues from self-policing to academic policy. Reputations are built on discovery, they are destroyed through aspersions of fraud. Much of this takes place in the nether world of professional societies, having next to nothing to do with larger public concerns. This volume, therefore, is concerned with the double life of social science: fraud and its impact on public confidence in and respect for the views and opinions of social scientists, as well as the way charges and counter-charges embroil the professional life of social scientists with the intimacies of their everyday private lives.

Irving Louis Horowitz

Acknowledgments

This volume had its origins in a "focused" issue of *Society* (volume 31, no. 3, 1994) which had as its theme fraud in research. Papers originally published in that issue have been joined by two prepared especially for this volume and others which first appeared in print elsewhere. Without the efforts of Irving Louis Horowitz, Howard Schneiderman, Brigitte Goldstein, and other members of the editorial staff of *Society*, this volume could not have come into being.

We arc grateful to the editors of the *American Scholar* and to the United Chapters of Phi Beta Kappa, its publisher, for permission to reprint David Goodstein's paper in this volume, which originally appeared under the title "Scientific Fraud" (volume 60, no. 4, 1991, pp. 505–15); and to the editors of *Academic Questions* and Transaction Publishers for permission to reprint James S. Coleman's paper, which originally appeared under the title "On the Self-Suppression of Academic Freedom" (volume 4, no. 4, 1990–91, pp. 17–22). Finally, we express our continuing gratitude to Eric Workowski of the Graduate School of Criminal Justice at Rutgers, who provided research assistance in a variety of areas for this project.

Nathaniel J. Pallone and James J. Hennessy

Part I

Deception:
Its Varieties and Its Engines

1

Deception, Fraud, and Fallible Judgment

Nathaniel J. Pallone and James J. Hennessy

This volume concerns itself with deception in the social and behavioral sciences and with social science perspectives on conditions that elicit deceptive behavior among scientists, whatever their discipline. As David Goodstein forcefully demonstrates in his chapter, the myth of the noble scientist has been severely challenged (or perhaps laid to rest), both in this country and abroad, in the wake of widespread public awareness of malfeasance among sometimes highly visible members of the scientific community. Episodes of misconduct in research once resolved or "handled" *in camera* within the academic or scientific community now command media attention on an unprecedented scale. One net effect over the long term may prove to be that public confidence in the research enterprise (and, concomitantly, public willingness to invest tax dollars in the support of that enterprise) has been irretrievably weakened. Another may be that the specter of public humiliation attendant upon the discovery of misconduct may constitute a deterrent extraordinarily more powerful by several degrees of magnitude than the relatively mild sanctions typically associated with *in camera* proceedings.

Since 1990, the press has reported, often in blaring headlines, a number of cases of real or apparent misconduct among members of the scientific community:

- As a result both of his failure to monitor the activity of a junior colleague and of what was widely interpreted as an effort either to minimize, to cover up, or to "stonewall" the situation, a Nobel Laureate resigns as president of one of the nation's most prestigious research universities. The junior colleague fabricated results that were reported in a research

3

paper. Although the Nobel Laureate had little to do with the study, he allowed his name to be affixed to the paper, which was published in a scholarly journal. *Science* (May 10, 1991) headlines its story: "Baltimore Throws in the Towel." More ominously, the *New Republic* (May 18, 1992) titles its account "The Science Mob."

- Systematic deception over a period of thirteen years surfaces when it is learned that a Canadian physician cooperating with researchers at a major U.S. medical school had reported fictitious results, on the basis of which the principal investigators had advised the medical community world-wide that a "less radical" surgical procedure than mastectomy had proven effective treating cancer of the breast. Although the principal investigators had learned of the deceit years earlier, they had not retracted their claims in favor of the "less radical" procedure. *Time* (March 28, 1994) headlines its report "A Diagnosis of Deceit."
- International litigation over patents erupts when a research scientist at the National Institutes of Health claims primacy in the discovery of the virus principally responsible for AIDS and for developing a blood-screening technique for its early detection likely to yield handsome royalties in the pharmaceutical market. The headline in *Science* (January 8, 1993): "NIH Scientist Guilty of Misconduct."
- Nearly a decade after they had, apparently knowingly, placed HIV-con-taminated blood stocks for sale on the world market (and distributed such stock without charge to hemophiliacs in their own country), a veritable Who's Who array of senior scientists in the French biomedical establish-ment is convicted of criminal wrong-doing. The *New York Times'* (Febru-ary 13, 1994) headline: "Scandal Over Tainted Blood Widens in France."
- Charges that a physician specializing in infertility performed artificial insemination using his own sperm rather than that obtained from prop-erly licensed sperm banks leads the *Washington Times* (December 21, 1991) to trumpet "Fertility Doctor May Be Father of 75 Children."

The misconduct alleged, whether "scientific" or "professional," in these celebrated cases derives from the biomedical sciences. But only slightly less notoriety has attended allegations of fraud or misconduct, whether scientific or professional, in the social and behavioral sciences:

- A psychologist specializing in the study of severe retardation admits to fabricating data which purportedly demonstrate the superiority of one class of pharmacotherapeutic preparations in controlling the potentially self-destructive behavior of retardates; again, the stakes in the pharmaceutical marketplace are high. He is convicted of falsifying research data. His misdeeds are discovered and reported by a fellow psychologist at another university; the "whistle-blower" later receives the American Association for the Advancement of Science Award for Scientific Responsibility.
- Charges of misconduct are leveled against a research psychiatrist con-cerning his studies of the effects of low levels of exposure to lead on the

cognitive development of children. After publication of that research fully a decade before misconduct is charged, the Centers for Disease Control had issued warnings about "danger thresholds" for lead exposure and the New York State legislature had enacted legislation that mandated statewide lead screening for pregnant women and young children, created a state registry listing all children with elevated lead levels, and established a Lead Poisoning Prevention Program within the State Department of Health; the social and economic costs associated with the policy implications of the research were thus massive. His accusers allege that, in the kindest reading, the psychiatrist had suppressed contrary evidence by "massaging" his data. The battle is waged in the press and in the courts as well as before scientific tribunals. The *Washington Times* (October 6, 1992), in a story headlined "Miscasting Lead as an Ecological Heavy," complains that "money that could be spent on the threat of malnutrition, poor education, disrupted communities, and the blight of drugs that infests America's urban centers is being redirected to focus on testing for lead."

- A former seminarian alleges that the cardinal-archbishop of the nation's largest Roman Catholic archdiocese had sexually molested him years earlier while he was attending a preparatory seminary. The allegation is spread widely through print and television journalism and yields a veritable bonanza for "tabloid" programs. Though the accuser later withdraws the charges, the episode represents the most sensational of the cases of civil and criminal prosecution that pivot on the so-called "clinical technique" of reconstructing (sometimes under hypnosis, sometimes under the administration of "truth serum") supposedly long-suppressed memories of childhood events which invariably result in the recollection of sexual abuse, frequently ritualized and sometimes even, in the judgment of one Harvard psychiatrist, perpetrated by extraterrestrial beings. The practitioners who specialize in this technique volubly and proudly describe themselves as "trauma-searchers" and are glorified as heroes and heroines in the never-ending search for covert atrocities in a panoply of trade books written by authors with weak scientific and academic credentials. The virtually universal judgment of the mental health sciences is that the "technique" constitutes sheer quackery and the establishment of a False Memory Syndrome Foundation to aid those accused as perpetrators in such "reconstructed" tales of past abuse (countered, to be sure, by a League of Lawyers for Survivors to press the claims of the accusers, at a fee of one-third the yield). Nonetheless, a judgment of $5 million has been levied against one such alleged abuser, while another serves a long prison sentence. Richard Ofshe and Ethan Watters analyze the genesis of the woeful situation in their chapter in this volume.
- Researchers at a major university refine a technique called "facilitated communication" that presumably enables autistic children to communicate at levels indicative of high intellectual functioning, including in some instances the production of poetry of publishable quality. Under this tech-

nique, a "communications assistant" holds the arm of the autistic child as he or she types on a keyboard-like device; the assistant takes care to insure that the content of the child's communication is in no way affected by his or her presence. The technique is greeted warmly by teachers, parents, and advocacy groups, and a major training center is established at the university. By the spring of 1993, the technique and its widespread adoption has engaged sufficient public attention that the Public Broadcasting Service's television series "Nova" produces an hour-long documentary entitled "Prisoners of Silence." Skepticism still pervades the scholarly community, where the prevalent view holds that controlled studies have failed to support the enthusiastic but unsupported claims made by proponents of the technique, a fact that PBS does not fail to notice.

It is a fair assessment that public confidence in the learned sciences and the learned professions erodes in direct proportion to the incidence and notoriety of such episodes. The flavor and perhaps depth of that skepticism can be gauged by the title syndicated writer Alston Chase chose for his column for October 7, 1991: "When Scientists Serve as Guns-for-Hire." Chase rather cynically predicted that, inevitably, the response of the scientific community would involve the emergence of the empirical study of the determinants of fraud and deception as a scholarly specialty, followed to be sure by proposals to fund research fellowships so focused. As an antiphon, *Time* devoted its cover story for August 26, 1991 to "Science Under Siege."

Smaller Stakes, Minor Misdeeds?

Misconduct in biomedical research that leads to direct harm to patients, or that raises unrealistic hopes for "miracle cures," is readily condemned as cruel and perhaps criminal. Not many events in psychological, sociological, or anthropological research either promise or deliver such cures; even cutting-edge research in the social and behavioral sciences has not yet reached the stage at which, in order to establish primacy of discovery in relation to patentable medications, devices, or procedures, findings are "published" via press conference rather than through the usual media for exchange of scientific information, a practice emerging in the biomedical sciences. The net effect of professional, as distinct from scientific, misconduct in the social and behavioral sciences is yet to be tolled.

In one of the few empirical studies of the relative incidence of serious misconduct across scientific disciplines, Princeton sociologist Patricia

Woolf (1988) found that 80 percent of the cases she investigated had occurred in the biomedical sciences and only 8 percent in the behavioral sciences. Woolf's 10:1 ratio is paralleled in the only public report (1992) issued by the Office of Scientific Integrity Review (an organization established in some large measure as a result of congressional reaction to revelations of the sort just litanized) of the U.S. Public Health Service, of which the National Institutes of Health is a component, and has since "merged" into the NIH-PHS Office of Research Integrity. Of the relatively miniscule number of cases of alleged misconduct in which OSIR had reached, during its entire life span, an adjudicatory determination of wrongdoing, 83 percent involved biomedical scientists, 8 percent physical scientists, and another 8 percent psychologists; no sociologists, anthropologists, historians, or policy analysts were either accused or adjudicated. The first (and as of this writing only) report of the Office of Research Integrity as its successor organization (1993) contains substantial more detail concerning complainants ("whistle-blowers") and their relationship to alleged wrongdoers as well as information about the sanctions meted out, either through NIH-PHS or institutional channels, but curiously does not specify the disciplines in which the wrongdoing was alleged or was substantiated to have occurred.

Some observers, including David Goodstein later in this volume, might attribute a relatively greater incidence of scientific misconduct in the biomedical (and the physical) than in the social-behavioral sciences to the relatively higher "stakes" at issue. A cursory glance at the aggregate annual research expenditures of federal funding agencies (e.g., the National Institutes of Health and its myriad subunits and the several Department of Defense agencies vs., say, the several National Endowments and the agencies concerned with health, education, and welfare) relevant to each set of disciplines lends support to such an interpretation. But the variant research ethos in the biomedical sciences, the physical sciences, and the social-behavioral sciences may also play a contributing role. In the social-behavioral sciences, with some rare exceptions, the research enterprise still proceeds largely according to the nineteenth-century Teutonic model: the solitary investigator, alone in his or her laboratory or study, focusing on an inquiry that is appropriately limited ("one-investigator-wide") in scope. This is not the case in the biomedical and physical sciences, where large teams of scientists in major laboratories, usually linked to each other in formal and informal national and international networks, address research issues of major scope and consume vast funds in the process. The latter ethos may provide more fertile ground for the rush to publish, the drive to establish primacy of discovery, the mutual aggrandizement of the members of one's own re-search team through inclusion among a list of authors on a scientific paper of some members who have made no contribution to the study whatever so as to optimize the prospect for continued or fresh funding, and the frank fabrication of data.

The fact is that we have, at national scope, few viable mechanisms either to monitor, codify, or sanction episodes of research misconduct across disciplines. At the federal level, the agency that most closely approxi-mates such a mechanism is the Office of Research Integrity within the NIH-PHS megalith, an organizational placement which virtually dictates that the complaints it receives, investigates, and adjudicates (or refers for prosecution) will be tilted strongly toward the biomedical sciences and, in essence, limited to scientists whose research funding has derived from the various subagencies within the megalith. Organizational entities with simi-lar purviews are not found in major federal funding agencies; instead, the various directorates within the specific agencies are implicitly charged with monitoring research misconduct, but without formal and organized mechanisms for so doing. They lack the scope and influence of the ORI, precisely because of NIH's pre-eminence as a dispenser of federal re-search monies, at least for investigations that are not "classified."

In June 1994, the National Academy of Sciences sponsored a convo-cation concerned (perhaps slightly euphemistically) with the "integrity of scientific research." Though peopled by conferees who included stel-lar names in the scientific enterprise, at least as recorded in a report in *Science* by Bruce Alberts, president of the National Academy, and Ken-neth Shine, president of the Academy's Institute of Medicine, the gen-eral thrust of the convocation's recommendations were relatively pale, emphasizing "preventative" approaches through mentorship, role mod-eling for young scientists and graduate students by senior persons of unquestioned probity, and perhaps even formal instruction in the ethics of the research enterprise. By implication, the tenor veered far from formal investigatory and sanctioning, especially through centralized authorities like the ORI.

Among the professional and scholarly associations in the social and behavioral sciences, the Ethics Committee of the American Psychological Association actively monitors and sanctions ethical violations, most often as a result of disciplinary action taken by a state licensure board. As reflected in the 1994 committee report, these tend to be cases of professional, rather than scientific misconduct, most frequently clustering around sexual liberties with clients, inappropriate fees, or advertising alleged to be misleading even by APA's enormously elastic standards. Indeed, only one (representing 1.5 percent) of the complaints received by the APA Ethics Committee alleged scientific misconduct, and that concerned an authorship controversy. To ward off the temptation to sanctimony as they compare themselves to their "clinical" brethren, scientific psychologists need only recall the devastating impact of Julius Seeman's (1969) analysis of experimental research in personality and social psychology, which clearly identified deception as the research methodology of choice from Sherif's and Asch's studies on social perception in the 1930s, through Festinger's investigations on cognitive dissonance and Krech and Crutchfield's on conformity in the 1950s, to Milgram's studies on obedience and Zimbardo's on the prisoner's dilemma in the 1960s. Seeman's work contributed directly to the inclusion of the social and behavioral sciences in the restrictions imposed by the then-emergent restrictive federal legislation on human subjects in funded research, originally targeted at the biomedical sciences, and effectively sounded a death knell for experimentation in personality and social psychology. If scientific deception among psychologists is today rarely brought to the attention of the APA, it may be because episodes of real or alleged misconduct are investigated and adjudicated at an "intramural" level by the institutional review boards in academic institutions and research centers subject to that legislation. Units in scholarly organizations in the other social and behavioral sciences with mandates similar to those of the APA Ethics Committee are neither so large, so well-organized, nor so active, perhaps because these sciences are not represented routinely in the arena of professional practice with direct client contact nor subject to state licensure.

Thus, one can only speculate about whether the cases of scientific misconduct that command media attention constitute the iceberg itself or merely its tip and about the distribution of misconduct among and between the several scholarly disciplines, whether across the sciences or across the social and behavioral sciences. The very lack of a coordinated set of mechanisms to monitor, codify, and sanction may itself reveal the normative expectation both within the scientific community and, until recently, within the public awareness that there is no need to police scientific misconduct because the very canons of science themselves preclude misbehavior and that the scientific enterprise is thus self-correcting. It is that expectation which the notoriety attached to "high profile" cases has challenged.

In May 1995, a federal court in Maryland awarded nearly $2 million in damages to a Cornell epidemiologist who charged that researchers at another institution had stolen her intellectual property by cribbing her research results—of which they had become aware during an early period of inter-institutional cooperative research—and incorporating them into a proposal forwarded to a funding agency without attribution as to source. However atypical or merely undetected such behavior may be, the significance of the case lay in the course which the aggrieved epidemiologist chose to pursue by opting not to invoke the mechanisms for monitoring scientific misconduct that operated within her own institution or that of the alleged plagiarizers, nor within the funding agency, nor with the relevant professional and scholarly organizations. Instead, she opted to seek redress directly through the courts, which had little difficulty in establishing ownership of intellectual property or in affixing substantial liability for scientific misconduct. As Taubes observed in the May 26 issue of *Science*, the case has been widely interpreted as a portent of things to come unless the scientific enterprise, and its myriad component disciplines, shows itself both willing and able to rigorously police misconduct within its own ranks.

Fallible Judgment, Misconstruing, and Dogmatism

As Robert Joynson suggests later in this volume, perhaps the first distinction to be made in an analysis of deception in the sciences is that between fallible judgment and deliberate fraud. At different times during the 1960s at NYU, we were privileged to participate in Professor William Gruen's course in the philosophy of scientific inquiry. Gruen was deeply committed to the proposition that the scientific enterprise, demonstrably and historically, contains self-correcting mechanisms. Rendering Averroës in a latter-day key, he insisted that today's widely accepted scientific truth might yet become tomorrow's quaint curiosity. Yesterday's psychoanalytic formulation that the classic anxiety neurosis issues invariably from a failure to resolve appropriately the Oedipus or Electra complex in childhood may yield tomorrow to precise knowledge of the effect of a particular neurohormone on mood and behavior gained through empirical investigation, relying on the CAT scan or MRI rather than through the reconstruction of childhood experiences via the interpretation of dreams.

One of Gruen's more memorable lectures concerned the utility of even patently false scientific theory in extending the frontiers of knowledge. He nominated as a principal exemplar of "fallible judgment" the theory of intra-atomic ether developed in nineteenth-century physics. The substance, inferred to "fill the spaces" between neutrons and protons in the atomic nucleus, was held to be, as a matter of definition, odorless, colorless, and without mass. But, since, as a matter of inferential necessity, it "must" exist, it was held to be possible to transmit electrical impulses through the substance. By 1930, Gruen declaimed, the theory of intra-atomic ether had irrevocably and univocally been demonstrated to be false; yet, he said, all the radios and wireless telegraphs in the world did not cease to function as a result of that account. Formulation of the theory of intra-atomic ether clearly constitutes a case of fallible judgment, yet one is hard-pressed to denominate it as a case of deliberately fraudulent behavior.

That is a very different matter from a situation in which a biomedical or behavioral scientist manufactures research data or claims to hold credentials he or she does not possess. The latter behavior rather clearly reflects the *intent to deceive,* while the former represents a (perhaps collective) error in inferential judgment. The genesis for fallible judgment may inhere in the state of the science itself (in nineteenth-century physics, pivoting on the principle of the conservation of energy and matter through mutual transformation, the notion of intra-atomic "emptiness" may have been inconceivable); in habits of minds that are exceedingly anthropocentric, leading to the misapplication of the paradigms of the past (as Robyn Dawes [1993] argues in a remarkable paper on the sources of misattribution in the pre- and post-diction of events); in fixed ideas dogmatically held by an investigator and enormously resistant to contrary evidence (as Mary Lefkowitz demonstrates in her discussion of the proposition that the ancient Greeks stole the seeds of civilization from even more ancient black Egyptians); or in personal and perhaps dogmatic political or cultural beliefs or values that would be irresistibly challenged by contrary judgments or interpretations (as Linda Gottfredson and James Coleman demonstrate in their chapters).

The central line of demarcation, then, between fallible judgment in the misconstruing of scientific evidence on the one hand and out-and-out fraud on the other may inhere in the *conscious* intention to deceive. But that line is clearly permeable: when I misconstrue data or err in the explanation of a social or psychological phenomenon perhaps as a function of ignorance of alternative explanatory constructs, but without the deliberate intent to deceive, I am guilty of fallible judgment; when I willfully and knowingly persist in broadcasting that misconstruction or erroneous explanation in the face of accumulated contrary evidence, however, I cross the point of demarcation. And, within the context of objectivity and public verifiability that constitute the *sine qua non* of scientific inquiry, willful persistence in fallible judgment may differ only in degree, not in kind, from the sheer fabrication of data or credentials.

Fraud as Intentional Deception

However else it may be construed (as, for example, the betrayal of a sacred trust or the violation of an ethical canon), fraud constitutes criminal behavior. Virtually universally, criminal codes define fraud as *the receipt of something of value under false pretenses*. Definitions both of "a thing of value" and "false pretenses" tend to be rather vague in those criminal codes, and perhaps intentionally so. Hence, the relevant law spans an enormous array of specific behaviors and their associated rewards.

When fraud is prosecuted and sanctioned through normal criminal justice procedures, the focal behavior generally consists of a rather blatant act that involves the eliciting of money by means of impersonation and can readily be detected by the mythic person-on-the-street or the cop-on-the-beat: the woman disguised as a nun, tin cup in hand, in a metropolitan railway station at holiday time; or the able-bodied man, also with a tin cup, posing as amputee outside the main entrance of an upscale department store. But when fraud consists of frank misrepresentation of the "product" one has to sell (or to give away) rather than misrepresentation of who one is, detection and prosecution typically flow along pathways substantially variant from normal policing procedures and depend to some extent on what used to be called "expert knowl-

edge." The cop-on-the-beat may be able to detect whether the suppli-
cant is genuinely a little sister of the poor or an amputee, but he frequently needs to rely on chemical analysis to discern the difference
between mineral oil and snake oil, and only a cadre of highly experienced accountants, auditors, and attorneys is likely to discover the difference between speculative but legitimate investment vehicles and
"Ponzi schemes." Or, in a somewhat hasty generalization, it may be that
fraud via impersonation is relatively readily detectable by the person-
on-the-street with a rudimentary knowledge of how to check credentials, while fraud via misrepresentation of product, whether snake oil or
shaky investments or research results predicated on fabricated data, is
inherently detectable only by those with specialized knowledge and/or
instruments of analysis.

Thus, it is no surprise that, in the "learned disciplines," allegations of
fraud have customarily been "policed" and prosecuted internally (according to rather informal and variable procedures) by the members of a
discipline itself; only rarely do we invoke the weight of civil authority in
the investigation or sanctioning of misrepresentation, either of person or
of product. Even when one has misrepresented himself or herself in a
flagrant act of "impersonation" (by, for example, claiming to have earned
an advanced degree) and has, on that basis, accepted salary or compen-
sation (surely a "thing of value"), the strongest sanction meted out is
typically dismissal, followed only in the rarest of circumstances by criminal prosecution. Hence, whatever public humiliation attaches to dismissal
represents, in general, the most severe sanction imposed for impersonation in the learned disciplines. Indeed, in a case that classically illustrates the tendency of institutions of higher education to infantilize faculty
members rather than hold them to standards of accountability typically
associated with adulthood, a popular (and tenured) professor in a major
university who had fraudulently claimed a doctorate was not only not
dismissed but was granted a paid sabbatical at institutional expense in
order to complete requirements for the degree he had fraudulently claimed
to have possessed for a dozen years.

Whatever the relative frequency or infrequency of the practice, fraud
by misrepresentation of product, whether through plagiarism or the fabrication or falsification of research data, similarly rarely merits a sanction more severe than public humiliation, which may ensue if one is
"barred" from participating in competition for research funds or if he or

she is forced to retract (or if the editors of the journal in which it has appeared themselves retract) a plagiarized article or research report. In a celebrated case that aptly illustrates what biologist Michael Ghiselin (1989), in *Intellectual Compromise,* labels "intellectual piracy," tenured associate professor "A" appropriated an unpublished manuscript that had been included in a packet of other credentials by an applicant for appointment at junior faculty rank at A's institution, then submitted the manuscript under his own name to a relatively obscure journal in his discipline. The aggrieved applicant, who had accepted appointment else-where, was startled to see her manuscript in print, under the authorship of A, a person with whom she had had only the most fleeting exchange during a visit to A's campus; she complained to the editors of the journal which had published the plagiarized piece. When the editors, after an investigation that unequivocally established authenticity of authorship, ceremoniously published a retraction and apology, the institution at which the plagiarizer enjoyed his tenured appointment threatened dismissal. But the dismissal of a tenured faculty member is a long and costly pro-cess; in the event, the plagiarizer was not only permitted rather quietly to resign but was provided a cash "bonus" in the form of a year's com-pensation for so doing, thus enabling the institution to "cost-avoid" the price of litigation. The plagiarizer had little difficulty in securing ap-pointment at another institution, where, in short course, he ascended to the chairmanship of the department.

The Axes of Deception

Deception by misrepresentation of one's identity or accomplishments (as in the case of claiming advanced degrees) or of the products of one's activity (plagiarism or piracy of another's data or manuscript or the frank fabrication of data) are but the most obvious varieties of deception that can be (and likely have been) perpetrated in the social and behavioral sciences. A classification of those varieties might proceed by consider-ing putatively deceptive behavior along four dimensions:

- First, the matter of *intent to harm.* Is the behavior at hand malevolent or benevolent? To misappropriate another's manuscript is fairly clearly ma-levolent; to affix a junior (or a senior, for that matter) colleague's name to the list of authors of a manuscript to which the colleague has made no contribution—perhaps because the junior colleague needs another publication to bolster the case for academic promotion, or perhaps because the reputation of the senior colleague may be expected to trigger more rapid acceptance for publication—is rather more benevolent. But both behaviors are intentionally deceptive.

- Second, the question of *reward*. Is the reward personal and tangible, or relatively impersonal and intangible? Achieving a higher salary or other emolument is clearly personal and tangible; enhancing one's reputation or status in the discipline is relatively less tangible.
- Third, the issue of who or what constitutes the *target or victim* of the deceptive behavior. The target may be fairly specific and personal (for example, the members of an academic committee considering an application for promotion in rank or of a peer review committee impaneled by a funding agency to advise on the merit of grant proposals) or relatively impersonal and intangible (for example, the untolled members of one's discipline, or the work of scholarship, or the universe of ideas).
- Fourth, the question of whether the deceptive behavior involves an *act of commission or an act of omission*. Fabrication of data is clearly an act of commission. At the opposite polarity stands the omitting of data or the failure to report results, either because they might undermine the neatness of one's conclusions or because they might prove, in today's climate, "politically incorrect." Quite nearby, however, one finds those cases which Ghiselin might label "deception by dogmatism": the educational researcher who fails to report that boys consistently achieve higher results in measures of aptitude or mastery in mathematics and science, or the psychiatric researchers who reported in the prestigious *New England Journal of Medicine* the apparently startling (to them) revelation that homicide occurs more frequently in municipalities with a high incidence of acknowledged gun ownership while utterly ignoring the substantially stronger association between racial mix and death by violence (or the interactive mix between gun ownership and racial composition) in those very communities. In the first instance, one assumes that allegiance to the dogma of gender equality is paramount; in the second, the dogma that a pluralistic society should blind itself to the consequences of racial and economic status confounds suggests itself as the governing variable. In a remarkably candid and virtually unparalleled self-revelation, renowned sociologist James S. Coleman acknowledges, in his chapter in this volume, that he and his associates overlooked significant data in the fabled study of the mid-1960s that demonstrated that black students of comparable ability do not do as well academically in segregated schools as they do in integrated schools (the first "Coleman Report"). Coleman writes that they failed to pursue data that had led them to conclude that "a major source of inequality of educational opportunity for black students [in segregated schools] was the fact that they were being taught by black teachers" who were demonstrably less competent, on average, than the teachers who taught otherwise similar black students in integrated schools. To have emphasized that finding would have violated a pivotal belief that

FIGURE 1.1
Axes of Deception in Relation to Characteristics of
Deceptive Behaviors and Their Likely Sequelae

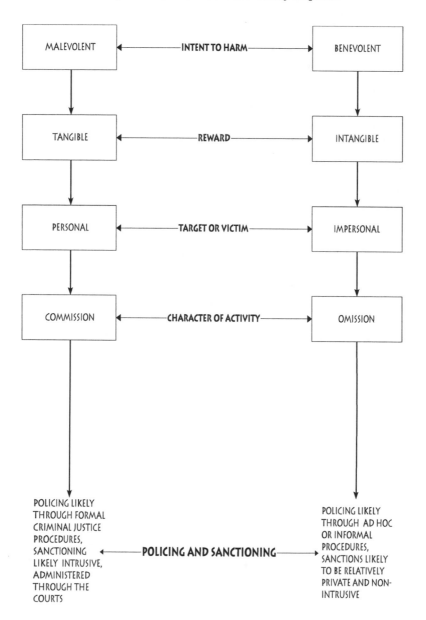

drove many of the Great Society programs of that era; and, besides, those less competent black teachers were, in the main, themselves the product of segregated education. Had self-suppression not prevented the broadcast of that finding, social policies favoring "forced" school integration by means of busing (along with the concomitant if unintended destruction of the neighborhood school) might have given way to social policies demanding the rapid improvement of academic quality in "historically black," separate but clearly not equal, colleges and universities—a matter that waited for redress until the 1993 Supreme Court decision in the Alcorn A&M case more than a quarter century later. And the 1972 siege of Boston, which further polarized racial conflict in that city, might not have occurred.

Those behaviors that fall along one set of polarities—malevolent in intent, aimed at tangible reward, targeted at a specific personalized victim, involving an act of commission—are relatively more likely to be pronounced to be cases of fraud; the policing or regulation of such behaviors are more clearly liable to formal criminal justice procedures, even if these procedures are only rarely engaged, and the sanctions are relatively more liable to be intrusive and "public." Alternately, those behaviors that are relatively more benevolent, produce only intangible reward, target no personal victim, and involve an act of omission rather than commission are much more likely to be regarded with no greater sense of opprobrium than that which attaches to the taxpayer who massages every rule in the IRS book to his advantage. They will be policed only through informal and ad hoc procedures, whether institutional or discipline-wide; sanctions are similarly likely to be relatively private and nonintrusive. We will have little hesitancy in pronouncing one set of behaviors as fraudulent in a formal sense and as meriting censure or formal criminal sanction at worst; we are likely to regard the other set as slightly less than honorable but hardly criminal. Yet the level of deception may be equally great and in some cases even more pernicious in its social policy ramifications.

Advocacy Research as a Funding Agency Priority

No effort to categorize the sources of deception in social and behavioral research can pretend to be complete without acknowledging deception, which arises not from the motivations of the individual scientist but rather from the advocacy stance of a funding agency. There can be little debate that no individual scientist is entitled to have his or her research supported, however much he or she is guaranteed freedom to pursue inquiry. Similarly, there can be little debate that a funding agency has the right to set its own priorities, which may or may not coincide with those of individual scientists or of the research community. Questionable practices arise, however, when the agenda that drives the funding agency remains covert, or when the agency vetoes certain variables as targets of free inquiry.

- During the 1950s, the Office of Naval Research rather unexpectedly undertook to fund a series of studies concerning the dynamics of cross-race work groups. In the main, the social and behavioral scientists who conducted those studies examined such work groups as teams of waiters and chefs in restaurants, hospital workers, and grounds keepers. Many claimed not to understand that ONR's interest lay not at all in integrating the civilian work force but rather in integrating the crews of atomic submarines which remain below ocean surface for months on end. Though the scientists involved were deceived by the funding agency as to its intent, the social science community generally approved that its research endeavors assisted in implementing what it regarded as a laudable social goal.

- Especially since the student revolt of the late 1960s has eliminated secret research on all but a relative handful of university campuses, by now Project Camelot may be but a distant memory (Horowitz, 1971). But in the late 1950s and early 1960s a number of social scientists undertook studies to identify emergent leadership in developing countries, doubtless from worthy motives. Most expressed chagrin when they learned that their studies had apparently contributed to the "neutralization" of those leaders whose political views were not in consonance with those of covert agencies of the U.S. government, and the social science community was appalled.

- Between the adoption of Federal Equal Employment Opportunity legislation and the emergence of affirmative action as a constitutionally acceptable avenue to correct historic wrongs, for roughly a decade federal agencies categorically forbade inquiry into race, whether in application for academic employment or student admission or, with very few exceptions, as a variable in federally-supported research. In the mid-1970s, consonant with then-prevalent federal policy, we were instructed not to include race as a variable in an investigation of the bases on which correctional administrators make decisions concerning custody levels of prisoners; ours was not an isolated instance. Members of the social science community aware of the prohibition of research on race were divided in their attitudes. Some, rather wistfully, opined that, since race should not matter, it ought not to be investigated; others believed that such studies could but reveal only a part of the truth and that the results of research thus constrained could not avoid misinforming.

- By the early 1990s, the pendulum had moved, but not swung. The University of Maryland submitted a proposal to NIH to gather a conference of genetic scientists focused on genetic factors in criminal violence; NIH's Human Genome Research Center awarded the grant. When the impending conference became public knowledge, a storm of protest arose in the Congress and elsewhere; the conference was canceled. In this case, the agenda of the funding agency seemed to conflict directly with a laudable social aspiration. The Maryland conference may be but the first casualty; may the Genome Center itself be the next?

If a single thread ties these cases together, it is that of fallible judgment originating from outside rather than from inside the research enterprise, motivated by convictions that societal needs or society's overarching agenda must perforce channel scientific inquiry. The burden of knowledge that is momentarily inconvenient may thus be avoided. But whether generated from the inside by petty motives or imposed from the outside on the basis of higher purposes or lofty aspirations, deception remains deception; neither society nor science can be well served thereby. Therein, indeed, may lie a unique role for the social sciences, as Marcel LaFollette argues in her chapter, and in a manner consistent with the proposals of the conferees brought together by the National Academy of Sciences—a role not defensively exculpatory but rather focused on the dynamics of positive socialization, not merely for our disciplines or for the sake of our colleagues in the "hard sciences," but for the welfare of society itself.

Recommended Readings

Bruce Alberts and Kenneth Shine. "Scientists and the Integrity of Research." *Science* 266 (1994): 1660–61.

Nachman Ben-Yehuda. *Deviance and Moral Boundaries*. Chicago: University of Chicago Press, 1985.

Robyn M. Dawes. "Prediction of the Future versus an Understanding of the Past: A Basic Asymmetry." *American Journal of Psychology* 106 (1993): 1–24.

Michael T. Ghiselin. *Intellectual Compromise: The Bottom Line*. New York: Paragon House, 1989.

Michael J. Mahoney. *Scientist as Subject: The Psychological Imperative*. Cambridge, Mass.: Ballinger, 1976.

Irving Louis Horowitz. "Social Science, Yogis, and Military Commissars." In Irving Louis Horowitz and Mary Symons Strong, eds., *Sociological Realities*, 522–31. New Brunswick, NJ: Transaction Publishers, 1971.

David J. Miller and Michel Hersen. *Research Fraud in the Behavioral and the Biomedical Sciences.* New York: Wiley Interscience, 1992.

Julius Seeman. "Deception in Psychological Research." *American Psychologist* 24, no. 11 (1969): 1025–28.

Patricia K. Woolf. "Misconduct in Scientific Research." *Jurimetrics Journal* 29, no. 1 (1988): 67.

2

The Fading Myth of the Noble Scientist

David Goodstein

Scientific fraud has become a very hot topic. Most scientists have traditionally believed that fraud in science is rare or nonexistent, but today there are congressmen and journalists and others who think otherwise, and even some scientists are not entirely sure. Confusion arises because, except in the most extreme cases, no general agreement exists on what constitutes fraud or serious misconduct in science. Furthermore, the public's perception of what scientists do and why they do it is distorted by myths happily perpetrated by the scientists themselves, with the consequence that normal and even essential forms of behavior by scientists can be viewed as sinister by those searching for evidence of wrongdoing. And, of course, there are indeed real cases of fraud in science.

Perhaps the most famous incident of scientific fraud in this century was the case of the Piltdown man—a human cranium and ape jaw that were found in a gravel pit in England in 1908 and 1912. Substantial academic reputations were made by discerning human characteristics in the jaw and ape characteristics in the cranium before this putative missing link was exposed as a fake in 1954. Another famous case was that of Sir Cyril Burt, a psychologist who worked on the heritability of intelligence by studying identical twins who were separated at birth and brought up in different environments. Unfortunately, there were very few cases of such convenient subjects for research, so it was charged that Burt obligingly invented thirty-three more and further helped matters along by inventing two assistants to help him study them. Burt died in 1971, three years before the charges were made.

In 1974 William Summerlin of the Memorial Sloan Kettering Center in New York was doing research that required nature to produce for him some rats with healthy black patches grafted on their skin. Since nature was not sufficiently cooperative, he helped her along with a black, felt-tip pen and was caught in the act. In another case, John Darsee, a prodigious young cardiologist at Harvard Medical School, was publishing approximately a hundred papers a year. Until he was caught red-handed fabricating data in 1981, it did not occur to anyone that with that rate of production maybe he didn't have time to do the actual experiments. In yet another case, Stephen Breuning made headlines in 1987 when it was revealed that he had fabricated data in his research at the University of Pittsburgh on the effects of psychoactive drugs in children.

The most recent notorious case involves the Nobel Prize-winning biologist David Baltimore, former president of Rockefeller University. A post-doctoral researcher named Margot O'Toole, without accusing anybody of fraud, claimed that the evidence did not support the conclusions in a paper written by Baltimore and a number of his collaborators. The events that ensued would have served nicely as a plot for Euripides. Baltimore used his immense prestige to rally the scientific community behind him, facing down investigations at two universities and in Congress. When evidence emerged that one of the authors, Tereza Imanishi-Kari, needing to substantiate what Baltimore was loudly declaiming, had fabricated data to shore up the case *after* the initial investigations, Baltimore still didn't back down, claiming that what she wrote in her notebooks was her private affair, so long as it wasn't published. This attitude, when it finally came out in the report of yet another investigation, shocked even Baltimore's staunchest supporters. The final act of this scientific drama is likely to be cathartic for science, and perhaps even satisfying to members of Congress.

The first serious congressional attention to scientific misconduct seems to have come in 1981 when the investigations subcommittee of the House Committee on Science and Technology was prompted to look into a Harvard Medical School case. Albert Gore, then representative from Tennessee, was chairman of the committee. Philip Handler, then president of the National Academy of Sciences, made a presentation to the committee in which he told them, more or less, that this was something beyond their understanding and that they should keep their grubby hands out of it. Handler's view was not exactly well received by Congress, whose members felt that the scientists, after all, were being supported by the public and ought to accept congressional oversight. Nevertheless, these hearings did not lead to any congressional action. During the early 1980s, Orrin Hatch, Republican senator from Utah, started poking into the National Cancer Institute, also without permanent effect. But more recently and with greater publicity, two Democratic representatives, John Dingell of Michigan and Ted Weiss of New York, held hearings in their respective subcommittees on the Baltimore case. Dingell had inherited Gore's subcommittee on science and technology, and Weiss was head of the subcommittee on human resources and intergovernmental relations of the Government Operations Committee. Dingell's hearings had considerable influence, but they don't seem as yet to have produced any formal result. Last October, Weiss's committee issued a booklet containing an analysis of ten cases of scientific fraud entitled "Are Scientific Misconduct and Conflict of Interest Hazardous to Our Health?" The booklet is especially critical of the universities for their handling of these cases. The committee report was not well received in the press, which pointed out that it was based largely on an analysis of cases that had occurred in the early 1980s, and that much has changed since then. The report seems to have dropped out of sight.

Meanwhile, at the National Institutes of Health, two staff biologists named Ned Feder and Walter Stewart set themselves up as a kind of self-appointed truth squad. According to their critics, they had not been very productive scientists and were trying to find a way of holding on to their laboratory and office space. They hit upon the fraud issue and were particularly visible in the Baltimore case. In other cases, too, they have become the point team for whistle blowers. Feder and Stewart now have official permission from their superiors to spend a certain percentage of their time pursuing wrongdoers.

In 1988 and 1989, the National Institutes of Health (NIH) and the National Science Foundation (NSF) each published in the *Federal Register* formal sets of regulations regarding scientific fraud. These two sets of regulations, many pages long, are virtually identical. Both of them call on the university (if the fraud has been committed at a university) to investigate the situation first and only later to hand it over to the agency. A rule was declared late in 1989 by the Public Health Service (PHS), the parent organization of NIH, stating that after January of 1990 no research proposal would be accepted from any university that did not certify that it had in place a formal set of regulations about how to handle research fraud. Suddenly, every research university in the country had to have a formal set of regulations for dealing with scientific misconduct. An Office of Scientific Integrity (OSI) has been established within NIH. The NSF does not yet have such an office, but they have an inspector general who would seem at first glance to serve much the same function. However, it turns out that the staff of the new OSI see themselves in a different and somewhat surprising light.

In the spring of 1991, after a year's operation, OSI took its show on the road to address the wider academic community and to assess the year's work. In Seattle, where I saw them, the theme of their presentation was, we're the friendly folks from OSI, and we're here to help you. "The question," said Dr. Jules Hallum, director of OSI, "is, can science police itself?" By that he meant, can the job be done by OSI. The staff of OSI are nearly all Ph.D. scientists, and they see themselves not as a part of the government bureaucracy but as part of the scientific community. Coincidentally, it was during the same week as the Seattle meeting that news broke about the OSI investigation that finally undermined Baltimore's defenses.

At the Seattle meeting (where the audience was largely scientists-turned-administrators from West Coast universities), as at the earlier Washington, D.C., meeting (where the audience had mostly been D.C. lawyers), the most contentious issue that arose concerned the types of misconduct sufficiently serious to warrant OSI attention. In fact, OSI is careful not to use the word *fraud* at all, preferring instead the term *scientific misconduct*, defined in the Final Rule issued by the PHS as: "fabrication, falsification, plagiarism, or other practices that seriously deviate from those that are commonly accepted within the scientific community for proposing, conducting and reporting research."

By contrast, the regulations from my university, Caltech (to take a random example), define research fraud (purposely broader than scientific fraud) as "serious misconduct with intent to deceive, for example, faking data, plagiarism or misappropriation of ideas." There are two distinctions to note here. First, OSI steers clear of saying *fraud* because it doesn't want cases hung up on proving intent to deceive, an essential ingredient of fraud, whereas the Caltech rules assume that in such offenses as faking data, plagiarism, and misappropriation of ideas, intent to deceive is manifest. Second, whereas the Caltech regulations explicitly exclude from its domain transgressions less serious than those it defines as fraud, the PHS Final Rule casts a broad net with the phrase "practices...commonly accepted within the scientific community."

Even under the Caltech rules, however, research fraud is different from civil fraud. First of all, tort law envisions a plaintiff and a defendant; someone has to bring the case to court. In order to prevail, the plaintiff must prove five points: (1) that a false representation was made—in other words, that the defendant cheated; (2) that the defendant knew it was false (or recklessly disregarded whether it was); (3) that there was intent to induce belief in this misrepresentation; (4) that there was reasonable belief on the part of the plaintiff; and (5) that there was resulting damage. By contrast, all observers seem to agree that research fraud can be established without the help of a plaintiff who can prove that he has believed and been damaged by the misrepresentation that has been committed.

There may also be a more subtle difference between scientific fraud and civil fraud. Tort law requires that an untruth has been knowingly perpetrated and that belief in the untruth has damaged a plaintiff. However, in all of the cases of scientific fraud that I have looked at closely (and this includes two recent cases at Caltech), the transgression consisted in failure to follow proper scientific procedures. In every case, the point being made was firmly believed by the perpetrator to be the truth. Fraud typically occurs when a scientist, knowing with certainty the outcome that a particular experiment would have, finds it unnecessary to go to the trouble of actually performing the experiment. That is precisely what Cyril Burt, for example, is generally supposed to have done. Moreover, the Baltimore affair apparently got started when Tereza Imanishi-Kari asked Margot O'Toole to replicate an experiment, confident that O'Toole would provide the data that Imanishi-Kari had claimed to have already obtained. When O'Toole was unable to get the desired result, the curtain went up for the great drama that followed. If, in these cases, the investigators did indeed fabricate data to support what they believed to be the truth, the scientific community would agree without hesitation that they were guilty of scientific fraud. Nevertheless, they might not pass the first and second of the tests for civil fraud enumerated above—namely, that of knowingly or recklessly making a false representation. And, to make matters worse, one might argue that, if all scientists rigorously adhered to proper scientific procedure at all times, very little scientific progress would occur.

To understand this argument, let us turn to a journalistic account of the issue of scientific fraud. *Betrayers of the Truth,* published in 1982 by Simon and Schuster, was written by William Broad and Nicholas Wade. Both were reporters for *Science* magazine, and Wade is now on the editorial board of the *New York Times*. They are, in other words, respectable journalists. The book has an appendix entitled "Known or Suspected Cases of Scientific Fraud," which includes the case of Claudius Ptolemy, the Alexandrian astronomer in the second century A.D. who wrote the *Almagest,* upon which all of astronomy was based until the time of Copernicus. Broad and Wade claim that Ptolemy committed fraud because he could not possibly have made the astronomical observations he claimed he made. By techniques of archaeoastronomy—using knowledge of how the sky works to run it backwards to see what the sky looked like at a particular time in the past—researchers have found that the observations Ptolemy reports were not made in Alexandria in the second century A.D., but rather, at the latitude of Rhodes in the second century B.C. They conclude that the actual readings were taken by Hipparchus of Rhodes.

Another person on the list of "Known or Suspected Cases of Scientific Fraud" is Hipparchus of Rhodes, whose observations, Broad and Wade say, were actually made by the ancient Babylonians. Both accusations seem unlikely to be correct. If Ptolemy's observations correspond to the sky at Rhodes in the second century B.C., they were not made by the ancient Babylonians. Broad and Wade do not comment on this apparent contradiction.

In addition to Hipparchus and Ptolemy, Broad and Wade list among "Known or Suspected Cases of Fraud" Galileo, Newton, Dalton, Mendel, and Millikan. If one subtracts from the body of science the work of Hipparchus, Ptolemy, Galileo, Newton, Dalton, Mendel, and Millikan— and, of course, all that follows from their work—there would not be much left. Yet the journalists never consider the deeper implications of concluding that so much of our scientific knowledge is based on fraudulent work. Broad and Wade may have stood on the shoulders of giants, but they have not seen very far.

To see a bit further, it is helpful to look in detail at a couple of the cases Broad and Wade cite. Consider, for example, that of Isaac Newton. Newton explained the propagation of sound waves in air. Newton's theory was so good he was able to calculate the speed of sound and then compare it with measurements. When he did, they disagreed by about 20 percent. Before Newton's theory, there was no idea at all why sound propagates in air, so to have calculated the speed within 20 percent was an intellectual triumph of considerable proportions. Nevertheless, Newton was not content with the small discrepancy, because another part of his work, the law of gravity, was based on the implausible idea that two bodies could exert forces on one another instantaneously and at a distance with nothing but void between them. He argued that this strange idea had to be accepted because of its success in precise, quantitative accounts of the observations. But if precise, quantitative success is the test of science for gravity, so it must also be for the speed of sound. Therefore Newton had to explain the 20 percent discrepancy.

The real explanation for the difference has turned out to be that sound is adiabatic and isentropic, but Newton had assumed implicitly that it was isothermal instead. In other words, in a sound wave the temperature rises and falls, pushing the sound along a little faster than it would otherwise go. Newton didn't know about that effect, so he calculated the speed that sound would have if it were all at one temperature. That subtle difference would not be understood until the idea of entropy came up two hundred years later. Obviously Newton was not to blame for not anticipating it. He still had to have some explanation for the discrepancy, so he came up with all kinds of arguments that are now known to be wrong: there is water vapor in the air that for some reason doesn't participate in sound waves; he had ignored the space taken up by the molecules of air, and so on. He made little fixes until he finally got his theory in agreement with the experiment. It is not very different from what theorists do today; if you have a theory that doesn't quite agree with the experiment, you speculate on what might cause the small discrepancy. In hindsight, Newton's fixes are funny and his motive revealing. But fraud? No, it is not fraud.

Another example in Broad and Wade's book is Robert Andrews Millikan, Caltech's founder, first Nobel Prize-winner, first president, and all-around patron saint. The accusation is based on notations found in his laboratory notebooks, which are located in the archives at Caltech. I show these notebooks to my undergraduate students every year precisely because they illustrate how real scientists behave in the real world.

Millikan was measuring the electric charges of oil drops; he wanted to prove that the electron charge came in definite units—that it was quantized—and then he wanted to measure what that unit was. He had already made his preliminary measurements, and he knew the answer with some precision. Millikan had a rival, Felix Ehrenhaft, who believed that electric charge was a continuous rather than a quantized quantity. Ehrenhaft criticized Millikan's results, so Millikan went back to the laboratory to get better data to have ammunition against Ehrenhaft. Later on Millikan published a paper in *Physical Review* in which he says he is publishing the data from "all of the drops experimented upon during 60 consecutive days."

Millikan's notebooks, however, tell a different story. Each page has notations on one drop. Millikan would evidently spend a whole evening watching one drop go up and down in his electric field, measuring its speed, taking down data, making calculations, getting the result for the charge. He knew, of course, what result he expected. So in some cases he would write in red (everything else is black), "Beauty—Publish," or "One of the best I've ever had—Publish." And then on one page he wrote, "Very low—something wrong." And, of course, that one did not get published, in spite of the fact that he said he published everything.

Millikan did not simply throw away drops he didn't like. That would have been fraud by any scientist's standard. To discard a drop, he had to find some mistake that would invalidate that datum ("distance wrong," he wrote on that page). Every physics student learns the difference between errors, which are an inevitable component of all good data, and mistakes, which are human folly that must be expunged lest they contaminate the scientific record. Errors are lovingly analyzed in every experimental paper. Mistakes are discarded without comment. The oil-drop experiment was a difficult one that Millikan was now pushing to the limits of its precision. Even after years of experience with it, he was still capable of doing something wrong that would render an observation useless. If every scientist were obliged to publish every mistake, the literature would be so full of garbage it would be unreadable (it's bad enough as it is). Even worse, in Millikan's case, any mistake would seem like confirmation of Ehrenhaft's contention. So, when he got a wrong result, or when he could observe directly that a drop was not behaving properly, he would examine his apparatus to find his mistake so that he could fix it. It didn't count as one of the "drops experimented upon." Needless to say, when he got a result that agreed with his expectation within his expected limits of error, he did not try very hard to find some reason for throwing it away. This, too, is accepted behavior, even though it builds a real bias into the results. Millikan was not committing fraud. He was exercising scientific judgment.

It is worth noticing in these instances that both Newton and Millikan were motivated by the need to convince a skeptical world of what they perceived to be scientific truth. In both cases, inestimable damage to science would have been done had they not succeeded. Nevertheless, as noted earlier, perpetrators of real fraud also generally do so when they are convinced that they know the right answer to the scientific question they are investigating. Newton and Millikan did not commit fraud, and what they did do was necessary and important, but they shared something distressingly in common with those who have been truly guilty.

And it is true that some scientists have been guilty. Who are they? Sociologist Patricia Woolf did a study of twenty-six cases of serious scientific misconduct that surfaced in one way or another between 1980 and 1987. It turned out that, of these twenty-six cases, two were in chemistry and biochemistry, one was in physiology, two were in psychology, and twenty-one were in biomedical sciences. Furthermore, of the twenty-six, some seventeen were committed by M.D.'s rather than by Ph.D.'s. The conclusion seems inescapable that, at least in recent times, scientific fraud is largely biomedical fraud. The question remains: Why is that true?

One reason some have suggested is that there is more money in the biomedical sciences, and money corrupts. However, fraud in the form of plagiarism is not unusual in such fields as history, where very little money is to be found. The more important motivation, I think, is career pressure. In every case of science fraud I have looked at, somebody was advancing a career rather than seeking direct financial profit. But all fields, not only biomedicine, have career pressures. Some have suggested that, since the large majority of fraud perpetrators are M.D.'s rather than Ph.D.'s, perhaps it is because medical doctors are trained in a different sort of ethic from scientists—doctors are more concerned with the health of the patient than with scientific truth. Being brought up in this ethic might give one a different attitude toward what is permissible and what is not. I find that argument curiously unconvincing. Besides, a review of cases investigated by OSI in 1990 found eight of the guilty parties had Ph.D.'s, four M.D.'s, and two had both degrees. So M.D.'s may not be more guilty than Ph.D.'s in the long run.

Another theory has to do with the reproducibility of results. In physics and other fields where there is little fraud, people believe that experiments are precisely reproducible, in the sense that if somebody else goes into the laboratory and does the same experiment, the result will be exactly the same. That isn't really true. Real experiments are too hard to be repeated precisely, but the idea runs deep that things are causally related in a relatively straightforward way and are therefore reproducible. It would be foolish to fake a data point, because somebody else will repeat the experiment and find the data point in a different place.

Biologists, however, believe in something called biological variability. This means that if you perform exactly the same experiment on two different organisms of the same kind, you expect to get different results. Biological truth is more statistical, less precise and inexorable than scientific truth in physics is generally supposed to be. Perhaps this variability provides a veil under which biologists might sometimes think they can hide a bit of cheating.

My own judgment is that scientists are most vulnerable to the temptation to fake data when (1) they are under career pressure to produce something; (2) they think they know what the answer is and feel that going to the trouble of taking the data is superfluous; and (3) they think they are somewhat protected because experiments are not expected to be precisely reproducible. This last point applies more to the biomedical sciences than to the physical sciences.

Faking data is not the only form of serious research misconduct. Plagiarism and misappropriation of ideas are generally also recognized as serious transgressions. The 1990 review of OSI cases turned up two cases of people who had faked entries in their bibliographies and one person who listed fake co-authors on a book chapter. In physics, where other forms of misconduct are relatively rare, I have seen serious breeches of ethics committed under the cloak of anonymity by referees of journal articles and research proposals. Some people object to guest authorship (putting the boss's name on the paper even though the boss did not participate in the research), but the practice appears to be perfectly standard in some fields. The practice of publishing the same thing in two different journals is called self-plagiarism by those who would elevate it into the category of scholarly misconduct. An example is this chapter, which is adapted from an article that appeared in a Caltech publication, *Engineering and Science* (and later in the *American Scholar*). That article was not written by me, but instead was extracted by Jane Dietrich, the editor of *Engineering and Science,* from the transcript of a seminar I gave on the subject. Publishing a paper (three times) you did not even write yourself is a new, groundbreaking form of misconduct that doesn't even have a name yet.

Are we to take all these offenses seriously? To use the words of the PHS Final Rule, what are the practices "commonly accepted within the scientific community"? The self-image of most scientists, and I think the image held by much of the public as well, amounts to what I call the Myth of the Noble Scientist. The Noble Scientist is supposed to be more virtuous and upright than ordinary mortals, impervious to the baser human drives, such as personal ambition, and, of course, incapable of misbehaving in even the smallest way. The myth originates, I would guess, in the Baconian view of the scientist as a disinterested observer of nature. Although Francis Bacon's version of the scientific method has long since been discredited by philosophers and historians of science, it lingers in the public mind, and even some scientists continue to pay lip service to it. Reality, however, differs substantially from the Myth of the Noble Scientist.

No human activity can stand up to the glare of relentless, absolute honesty. We all build little hypocrisies into what we do to make life a little bit easier to live. Because science is a very human activity, hypocrisies and misrepresentations are built into the way we do it. For example, every scientific paper is written as if that particular investigation were a triumphant procession from one truth to another. All scientists who perform research, however, know that every scientific experiment is chaotic—like war. You never know what is going on; you cannot usually understand what the data mean. But, in the end, you figure out what it was all about and then, with hindsight, you write it up describing it as one clear and certain step after the other. This is a kind of hypocrisy, but it is one deeply embedded in the way we do science. We are so accustomed to it that we don't even regard it as a misrepresentation anymore.

Glossaries explaining the real meanings of terms found in scientific papers occasionally make the rounds of the laboratories. For example, "owing to difficulties in sample handling" really means something like "we dropped it on the floor." "It has long been known that..." means

"I haven't bothered to look up the original reference." "Typical results are shown" means "these are the best data I ever managed to get." This sort of wry self-parody only recognizes that scientific papers may disguise what really happened, even though they are supposed to be rigorously honest. Courses are not offered in the rules of misrepresentation in scientific papers, but the apprenticeship that one goes through to become a scientist does involve learning them.

That same apprenticeship, however, also inculcates a deep respect for the inviolability of scientific data. It teaches how one distinguishes the indelible line that separates harmless fudging from real fraud. For example, it may be permissible to present your best set of data and casually refer to it as typical, but it is not permissible to move one data point just a little bit to make the data look just a little bit better. All scientists would agree that to do so is fraud.

Emerging tendencies in science may make it even more difficult in the future for all scientists to agree on an unstated common standard of behavior. One is the fact that today approximately half of the science graduate students in American universities come from abroad. These students have no less honesty or integrity than our own natives, but they may not find it as easy to understand the unspoken transmission of values that somehow is supposed to take place between student and mentor in a scientific graduate education. Another reason is the increasing importance of the computer in scientific investigation. Computer simulations tend to blur the distinction between theory and experiment. They are computations that produce "data" that are something part way between reality and prediction. They tend to undermine the few clear distinctions that do exist between what is permissible and what is not. Furthermore, the routine use of computers to aid in real experiments also tends to undo the old standards. For example, the rules and procedures of OSI seem to envision a nineteenth- or early twentieth-century scientist, carefully taking notes in a notebook much like Millikan's (ink only, cross out mistakes, never erase, and so on). This quaint picture has little to do with today's science, in which experiments are often entirely run by computers (computer memories can't be crossed out, they can only be erased). In some ways, the computer is the ultimate embodiment of the Myth of the Noble Scientist.

The Myth of the Noble Scientist serves us poorly precisely because it obscures the distinction between harmless minor hypocrisies and real fraud. The PHS Final Rule is dangerous because it assumes there is a single set of practices commonly accepted by the scientific community and sets up a government agency to root out deviations from those practices. Nevertheless, fraud does sometimes occur in science, and universities were certainly poorly equipped to deal with it before the PHS and the NSF forced us to put our house in order and write down and adopt regulations. It is easy to predict that we will be seeing more cases of scientific misconduct for a while; the very existence of rules and regulations and bodies designed to cope with the problem tends to make cases emerge. I can only hope that we won't wind up arranging things in such a way as would have inhibited Newton or Millikan from doing his thing.

3

The Role of the Social Sciences in the Analysis of Research Misconduct

Marcel C. LaFollette

Between May 1986 and May 1989, subcommittees in the United States House of Representatives held six high-profile oversight hearings on "research misconduct"—that is, the fabrication, forgery, and misrepresentation of data and experiments, plagiarism, and misrepresentation of authorship during the proposing, doing, or communicating of research in the natural, physical, and social sciences. With the exception of Robert Sprague, who primarily described his efforts to blow the whistle on clinical psychologist Stephen E. Breuning, only one of the thirty-eight witnesses called to testify at these various hearings addressed the issue as a social scientist.

The social science perspective has also been neglected in subsequent legislative hearings and in most formal reports on the topic from scientific associations. Throughout the evolution of a controversy that, in fact, revolves around expectations for human behavior, the political debate has by and large ignored how social science theory and insight might be applied to understanding and resolving one of the American research community's most painful and emotional issues.

The failure to employ social science knowledge does not derive from social scientists' lack of concern about ethics. Quite the contrary, *Society* and other journals have, through the years, exposed and attempted to prevent deceptive research practices, breaches of confidentiality, and abuse of human subjects. Social scientists have led the public debate over data privacy and organizations like the American Psychological

Association have developed extensive codes of ethics to guide professional practice. Nor does the omission stem from weaknesses in the knowledge base, from a lack of applicable social science theory. Instead, this gap relates to physical and natural scientists' long-standing rejection of the intellectual legitimacy and authority of the social sciences and the messages they bring. Too often, during the political controversy over research fraud, leading physicists, chemists, and biologists (although, fortunately, by no means all) essentially stuck their fingers in their ears and attempted to shout down even conservative assessments of what was really happening. Too often, they rebuffed explanations that reminded scientists that they, too, can suffer from human failings or neuroses, or that revealed training, management, and reward systems in which the "slippery slope" has become a quick route to success.

Uneasy accommodations of disciplinary perspectives is nothing new, of course. Such attitudes influenced the 1940s debates surrounding establishment of the National Science Foundation, and have fueled many a floor fight in university senates. In academic hierarchies, sociology, psychology, and anthropology of science remain "second siblings," dismissed as frivolous or "soft," and criticized as antagonistic to "real" science, or else irrelevant to research management, communication, or training problems.

The consequences of ignoring social science knowledge in this particular debate went beyond mere intellectual narrowness however, for it left those struggling to cope with the problem—that is, the bureaucrats and policymakers who develop federal regulations, and the university administrators who investigate a steadily increasing flow of allegations—with an inadequate theoretical framework for understanding issues beyond the details of each specific case. Anecdotes and personal opinions shared by well-intentioned research administrators, attorneys, and victims became "evidence" that informed policy.

Time after time, some physicist would state definitively that the cases being uncovered represented only a few "bad apples" in an otherwise sound barrel, or a biologist would assert that excess stress and competition (or insufficient funding) "explained" the rash of misconduct cases bubbling to the surface, but few social scientists responded. Contributing to the impression that social science insight was unnecessary was a misplaced emphasis on the amount or frequency of misconduct as the crucial and all-important measurement. If we only knew how much fraud or misconduct exists, many people argued, then we would know whether the problem should concern us.

Perhaps this approach appeased quantitatively trained people searching for a quantitative explanation, but it relied on curious logic. As if, as a resident of the District of Columbia, I should suspend all concern, caution, or action regarding street crime until I knew definitively the percentage of criminals (or, presumably, potential criminals) among my fellow citizens. Up to a point, tracking the amount of robberies does assist crime prevention and increase citizen awareness, but the number itself is meaningless without context and further data. What if percentages are decreasing but more robbers are armed, or if most robberies occur at one particular location?

Focus on a single number distorted all aspects of the scientific misconduct debate; it became a red herring, derailing and discouraging attention to the system wide conditions that enable, facilitate, or accept unethical research misconduct. What we need to know—if we are really concerned about promoting honesty, rather than simply explaining dishonesty—are the circumstances in which actions occur. What types of people violate which norms? What group factors influence violations? At what stages of education or career are violations committed? And without understanding of what motivates conformity as well as deviance, even the most precise measurement of quantity of deviance is useless. This is exactly the type of linkage, however, that has been missing from the policy debate.

The ability to apply social science knowledge to the study of unethical research practices has also been severely inhibited by inaccessibility of primary data and other source material whereby theory can be tested. This situation has often forced social scientists to examine cases of research fraud and misconduct "under glass," lending credence to an image of them as frustrated scientists pressing their noses against the laboratory window but comprehending little of what goes on inside.

Sociologist Patricia Woolf has apparently been successful in obtaining interviews, but other social scientists who have written about the topic, such as Daryl E. Chubin and Allan Mazur, had to rely on public reports or hearings testimony. Hearings have, in fact, been a rich source of detail during this drought period; but they, too, have limitations, for the testimony has concentrated more on how frauds are accomplished technically than on motivations or on contributing social factors.

The desire for primary data about the extent of actual misconduct led several scientists (most notably through the years, Adil Shamoo and Drummond Rennie) to suggest an "audit" of the data behind published reports of research. Most such proposals have involved sampling journal articles or grants, and then subjecting raw data and laboratory records to scrutiny by experts who would check whether published conclusions fit work actually completed, and so forth. Although the idea has merit, social scientists know well that such a project would pose several difficulties. Success of the project would depend on voluntary cooperation by the subjects, who would be promised confidentiality if previously undetected error or fraud were discovered.

Assuring absolute confidentiality to research subjects is an uncertain game these days however, as demonstrated by a number of recent court rulings—for example, a sociologist instructed by a federal judge to release to oil company lawyers his unpublished, confidential data taken from residents near an oil spill, and another case involving data on how children respond to cigarette advertisements. In addition, an audit uncovered instances of fabricated data, could the investigators ethically allow those results to remain unchallenged in the literature? Social scientists have been confronting ethical issues for many years whenever they study illegal or socially sensitive behavior.

Availability of the primary records from actual cases is unlikely to change dramatically in the near future. The sensitivity and seriousness of misconduct charges have tended to justify conservative archival policies; moreover, many of those accused have neither been convicted nor have they admitted guilt, and so may understandably shy away from formal, on-the-record interviews. Such legal considerations, the confidentiality and privacy guidelines for preliminary investigations at universities, and the fear of lawsuits for slander or libel have significantly restricted access to information on this topic. Relying on the public record works well for those of us who study political reactions to fraud, where "face" is everything, but not for most other social scientists. To date, comprehensive interviews with accusers and accused have usually been obtained by journalists, who can gain the confidence of skittish subjects and ask questions whenever a subject is willing because they need not prepare elaborate protocols or obtain institutional review board approval before proceeding.

Until investigative and case records are open and the subjects more willing to grant interviews, the scientists whose lives have been splashed across the pages of *Science* and *Nature* will remain vague, mysterious creatures. We will have considerable technical information about how many cc's of this or that were or were not injected or measured, but know next to nothing about why the researcher did it and how detection was evaded. Without better access to primary records, we will also know little about how and why suspicions are initially raised, or what factors determine whether someone remains a bystander or blows the whistle. Where primary records are made available, access frequently depends on a personal connection between the record holder and the social scientist. For issues of such high emotional content, that connection may render objectivity impossible.

Some years ago, I was given access to extensive correspondence files relating to a twenty-year-old case in the humanities, an invaluable experience that provided a behind-the-scenes glimpse of how suspicions are raised and are then informally disseminated around a field, and how the tangled strings of professional relationships can inhibit fairness. Thanks to that reading, I saw how a single person can assume the role of "nemesis" and pursue someone outside the limits of any formal investigation. It was useful and educational to analyze these letters, but it was also a deeply troubling experience. In a strange twist of fate, I had been a guest (and was most graciously and generously received) at the accused's home the year before. After many years in other employment, the man had resumed his teaching career in another state and become a respected, well-liked member of a new university community.

As I read through the files, therefore, both the accused and his accusers (many of whom I had also met through the years) were flesh and blood figures, not newspaper cartoons. The bitterness, vengefulness, and self-righteousness that spilled from the folders was astonishing. There were no heroes here; no one smelled sweet. The motives for the original violation of scholarly norms remain a mystery. The accused's letters hinted at explanations that could have been followed up in interviews. It was rich, revealing material and would have made a lively book; but it was a book I could not write. The same factors that had gained me access also stripped away scholary detachment and introduced bias. Nevertheless, the experience left me firmly convinced of the usefulness of research into the emotional and psychological underpinnings of academic fraud.

In addition to these methodological constraints, social scientists have also tended to draw conclusions unpalatable to many scientists. For every assertion that scientists are 99.99999 percent honest, or that only a tiny fraction of articles in the Medline data base have ever been formally retracted and hence fraud is rare and attention to it irrelevant, there have been social surveys that point to a quite different conclusion.

Although straightforward and relatively unsophisticated in design, *New Scientist's* 1976 reader poll, taken by a one-page questionnaire which readers were asked to return within a month, provided important data at the time. The journal asked such questions as "Does intentional cheating warrant investigation?" and "Is your knowledge of intentional bias based principally on [direct personal contact, information from a colleague, the scientific grapevine, the media, or this article]?"

Also solicited were specific details on the number of incidents respondents had observed, what type, where it took place, how many people were involved, the age and gender of the suspect, and so on. The magazine received 204 responses "and a considerable correspondence." To his credit, Ian St.-James-Roberts, who wrote the *New Scientist's* analysis, resisted the temptation of broad conclusions from a small, self-selected survey, but 52 percent of the respondents reported knowledge of intentional bias by direct personal contact, and another 17 percent had learned of an incident through a colleague with direct contact. St.-James-Roberts predicted that "the inherent contradictions and pressures of scientific endeavor makes it unlikely that intentional bias will disappear spontaneously."

"Perhaps the most important consideration of all," he stated, "is whether, if science doesn't develop its own controls, some new revelation...will cause them to be imposed from outside."

The major surveys conducted in the United States since then have tended to address perceptions or suspicions of fraud, rather than ask respondents to reveal specific information about specific violations. Psychologist June Price Tangney's 1987 survey, for example, found that researchers did not regard "falsified data" as a widespread problem. But 32 percent of her respondents reported that they had "suspected a colleague of falsifying data" and another 32 percent suspected a colleague of plagiarism. Sigma Xi's 1988 membership survey included the question whether these scientists had "direct knowledge of fraud (falsifying data, misreporting results, plagiarism) on the part of a professional scientists," and 19 percent agreed either "emphatically" or "in substance."

The results of the most comprehensive survey to date, that conducted by Judith P. Swazey, Melissa S. Anderson, and Karen Seashore Louis, have been reported in *American Scientist* (November/December 1993) and the rsearchers' findings also reveal a perception within American universities of widespread and varied ethical problems. Swazey and co-workers carefully note that they measured not the frequency or amount but the "rates of exposure to" and perceptions of ethical misconduct. Their figure of "between six and nine percent" (of students and faculty in chemistry, civil engineering, microbiology, and sociology) who "report that they have direct knowledge of faculty who have plagiarized or falsified data" is a far cry from *New Scientist's* 52 percent. Most likely, it reflccts not only improvement in survey methodology but also probably greater sophistication among respondents who have been exposed to debate about misconduct and are therefore more cautious about labeling activity as suspect.

Even more instructive than the Swazey group's data, however, has been the early reaction to it, most notably, statements by a few prominent scientists who attempt to dismiss its usefulness and validity because it did not measure the actual frequency of misconduct. As with much of social science research, in fact, the substance of the Swazey survey data lies in the detailed picture it paints of the social structure of the problem. For example, faculty report "striking differences between their espoused values and the actual practices in their department" on such vital issues as collective responsibility for educating students about good practice or for monitoring ethical behavior. The data reveal troubling levels of reported exposure to racial, ethnic, and gender discrimination, as well as widespread laxity in authorship practices.

The greatest contribution to understanding why otherwise brilliant and accomplished young scientists break the norms for acceptable conduct in their field may come when surveys are interpreted in the context of general theories of sociology and psychology. In the 1970s and 1980s, several scholars did explore the relevance of general theory to the topic of research misconduct but these writings received relatively little attention outside the social science community.

Now that the landscape is more detailed, and the importance of such understanding perhaps a bit clearer, it is instructive to return to four of those writers. Harriet Zuckerman's articles in the late 1970s and mid-1980s, for example, examined "deviant behavior in science" as a departure from cognitive norms (shared expectations) and social or moral norms (shared prescriptions, proscriptions, and permissions). She placed that behavior in the context of social control in science and examined the connection between behavior, control, reward structures, and competition for recognition.

Deena Weinstein, in a 1979 review of sociological theory related to scientific fraud, published in *Social Science Quarterly*, drew attention beyond the norms themselves to the conditions leading to their erosion, the barriers to enforcement, and the social consequences of violations. Her conclusions of the ineffectiveness of "personal policing" and the consequences on behavior of increased competition for scarce resources bear reconsideration.

In 1984, James A. Knight, a professor of psychiatry, discussed scientists' "compromise of ethical principles" in a *Perspectives in Biology and Medicine* article. Writing before the sensational cases involving Nobel laureates erupted, Knight focused on the role played by genius and creativity. He linked some scientists' striving for power and prestige to their perpetual fear and anxiety of failure, which he observed might lead even the most accomplished person to assure success "by hook or crook." Knight also outlines how one might study the link between moral development and elite status.

This theme of "deviance among the respectable" was also explored in 1985 by H. Kenneth Bechtel and Willie Pearson in a *Deviant Behavior* article. They pointed out then that "deviance that involves the actual practice of the scientific craft has been largely ignored, partly owing to its assumed non-existence, but also because deviance in one's own family is the last to be recognized or acknowledged." Deviance by elites is harder to study, and easier for elites to discourage. Bechtel and Pearson make a compelling case for a "sociology of scientific deviance," which exploits Robert K. Merton's theory of anomie by "placing the primary motivation toward deviance on the frustrations encountered by those who are expected to achieve, even told to achieve, but lack legitimate resources to be successful."

Viewing research misconduct as deviance—a term that has objective clarity for social scientists but can seem disturbingly value-laden to others—may have been good social science but, for all-too-human reasons, it served as red flag, last straw, and acceptable justification for ignoring the application of social science theory to an emerging problem.

Social scientists can continue to fold their arms and sit out the dance, of course, pretending that the distances between the disciplines make it nearly impossible to change the situation described. Research misconduct is a social science problem. Unethical research and professional conduct occurs throughout the university, in all fields, from civil engineering to sociology. The newly instituted political remedy—federal regulation—affects all disciplines because it applies to all disciplines, even those in which instances of fraud and fakery have been "rare." And this is also an intellectual problem to which social science expertise and knowledge can and should be applied. Responsible social scientists should regard applying that knowledge not as an option but as a social obligation.

Part II

Advocacy Scholarship and the Refraction of Truth

4

Miscounting Social Ills

Neil Gilbert

Social policy deliberations have become muddled in recent years by an increasing tendency among advocates for different groups to generate vast and often questionable estimates of social ills afflicting their clients. Advocacy research has not always been that way. The development of social welfare policy in the United States has benefitted from a long and honorable tradition of advocacy research—studies that seek to measure social problems, heighten public awareness of them, and recommend possible solutions. At the start of the twentieth century, studies intended to spur social reform focused upon the problem of poverty and its attendant miseries of slum housing, poor health, hunger, and child labor. Robert Hunter's book Poverty, first published in 1904, was an early classic in the advocacy research genre. Taking $460 a year as the poverty index for an average family of five in the Northern states and $300 a year in the South, Hunter estimated that at least ten million Americans (about 13 percent of the population) lived in poverty.

More than half a century later, in an era of relative prosperity, public concerns about poverty were revived by another classic, Michael Harrington's *The Other America*. Harrington reviewed estimates that showed between forty and fifty million Americans (20 to 25 percent of the population) living in poverty. His research concluded that a basic attack on poverty was necessary. "All that is lacking," he observed, "is political will." Harrington's work is often credited with having furnished moral impetus, along with an empirical case, for the Johnson administration's "war on poverty" in the 1960s.

Michael Harrington and Robert Hunter came from the same breed of advocacy researchers. Both men had spent time on the front lines as social workers, were drawn to socialism, and, while well versed in the social sciences, their studies embodied a felicitous combination of reportage and analysis that was highly accessible to the general public. Indeed, it might be said that their prose was as persuasive as their numbers.

Reflecting on his approach to the study of poverty, Harrington offers a candid account of the style and nature of advocacy research: "If my interpretation is bleak and grim, and even if it overstates the case slightly, that is intentional. My moral point of departure is a sense of outrage, a feeling that it would be better to describe it in dark tones than to minimize it."

This is not to say that his statistics were invented or misrepresented. Harrington explicitly identifies the assumptions and definitions that underlay his reading of the numbers. He readily admits that legitimate differences in point of view give rise to other definitions and interpretations, which yield different counts. And he reviews these alternative estimates of poverty in a balanced manner. Two principles guided his study *The Other America*: "To be as honest and objective as possible about the figures; to speak emotionally in the name of the common humanity of those who dwell in the culture of poverty." Joining unbiased measurement with committed expression of concern represents a standard of advocacy research at its best—a standard that has eroded with the increase in this activity since the 1960s.

Erosion of Standards

Following Harrington's study of poverty in the early 1960s, a notable rise in the volume of advocacy research was accompanied by an equally notable change in style and focus. As social rights for different interest groups expanded and public expenditures for new social programs climbed, an unprecedented level of federal funding became available for social research. With millions in research funds distributed among federal agencies such as the Administration on Aging, the National Institute of Mental Health, the National Center on Child Abuse and Neglect, the Department of Housing and Urban Development, and the Children's Bureau, the research focus shifted from the poor to diverse constituencies of the oppressed and deprived who claimed entitlements to social protection; they included women, gays, minorities, children, elderly, homeless, disabled, and those suffering various addictive behaviors. Along with an infusion of research funds that began with the Great Society programs in the early 1960s, the expansion of social research gained impetus from computer technology and new analytic tools that promised to inform policy debates with useful data. These developments were quickened by the tremendous growth in the number of professionals trained to conduct social science research. By the late 1960s, social scientists came to play an increasing role as advocates in the social welfare policy arena.

With the growing involvement of social scientists, the results of advocacy research measuring those in need became more questionable, and the prose less elegant. Accuracy of their estimates of need likewise became more questionable, in part, because some of the emerging problems were harder to gauge than poverty. The measurement of homelessness does not lend itself to conventional social science sampling methods using telephone interviews or door-to-door surveys; unlike poverty, problems such as racial and gender discrimination, child abuse, elder abuse, and drug abuse involve crimes that are difficult to uncover by surveys.

Also, expansion of social welfare program benefits for various groups produced lively competition, increasing pressure to inflate evidence of need for program support. Competition for funds is less of an issue when the more inclusive problem of poverty is being measured. Figuring the national incidence of poverty, for example, Harrington was not concerned if an error in his calculations might show that the number of poor were ten million less than he estimated. After all, he insisted, "give or take 10,000,000, the American poor are one of the greatest scandals of a society that has the ability to provide a decent life for every man, woman, and child." But as advocacy research has come to focus on problems more discrete than poverty, its function of promoting public awareness is being compromised by the growing tendency to greatly magnify needs while asserting the scientific validity of these large numbers.

Emotive Statistics

The expanding volume and declining quality of advocacy research has spawned the use of emotive statistics—startling figures that purport to document "hidden crises" and "silent epidemics." Frequent reports in the media lend authority to these figures as they are brought to national attention.

Consider the story in *The Los Angeles Times* (July 2, 1990), for example, reporting on a study of 32,000 California children in which 25 percent of those surveyed said that "they had gotten away from someone trying to kidnap them." Is it conceivable that one in four children or almost one child in every other family was a victim of attempted kidnapping? On a little reflection, most people would find it difficult to take these figures seriously, but not the professor of social work who conducted the study. In his view, the survey results indicate that California's extensive statewide program to provide children with training to prevent sexual abuse "is effective in teaching youngsters how to deal with the threat of physical and sexual abuse."

In the mid-1980s, fear of kidnappings was intensified by the widely publicized estimate that 50,000 children were being abducted by strangers annually. According to Child Find, an organization devoted to the plight of missing children, only 10 percent of these children were recovered by their parents, another 10 percent were found dead, and the remaining 40,000 cases per year remained unsolved. Prominently reported by the media, these figures first provided sensational headlines that proclaimed a national crisis. Later they became the grist for a Pulitzer Prize winning analysis of the problem in the Denver Post, which criticized the risk of child abduction as recklessly inflated. The *Post* revealed an astonishing discrepancy between the 50,000 estimate put forth by crusaders for missing children and the official number of FBI investigations of children abducted by strangers, which totalled sixty-seven cases in 1984.

A closer analysis of these figures by Joel Best in *The Public Interest* shows that if the advocates' estimates of 50,000 are too high, the FBI count of 67 is too low. The FBI's jurisdiction in kidnapping cases is limited to offenses that violate a federal statute, such as transporting a victim across state lines. Only a fraction of the cases reported to local law enforcement authorities come under the Federal Kidnapping Statute. Best demonstrated, on the basis of data from a study by the National Center for Missing and Exploited Children, which included police records on every reported crime in 1984 that involved kidnapping or attempted kidnapping of children in Jacksonville, Florida and Houston, Texas, that a reasonable extrapolation of serious incidents would yield a nation-wide estimate of 550 cases annually—about eight times higher than the FBI count, but still ninety times lower than the incidence rate claimed by advocates.

In defining the serious incidents of stranger abductions, Best considered only those cases that involved either murder or a child missing for more than one day. This definition coincides with the image of child abduction originally portrayed by advocates who promulgated the figure of 50,000 missing children, reported by ABC news and other sources. Researchers at the National Center for Missing and Exploited Children (NCMEC) employed a broader definition that included attempted kidnappings and cases in which the victim is missing for less than twenty-four hours. Use of the NCMEC definition in extrapolating a nationwide rate from the Jacksonville and Houston data yields a figure of 15,000 abductions by strangers annually.

But as Best points out, in the enlarged definition subscribed to by NCMEC researchers 97 percent of the cases involved a child missing for less than twenty-four hours and over 60 percent of the cases were crimes of molestation, (short-term abductions in the course of which the victim was moved to a different place); indeed, only 15 percent of these cases were classified as kidnappings or abductions by the local police. Sexual molestation is a tragic experience for its victims, but it is a crime very different from the kidnappings initially portrayed by advocates who claimed that 80 percent of abducted children continue to be missing each year. By including cases in which most victims are missing less than one day, the broader definition of child kidnapping advanced by the NCMEC and other missing-children advocates generates a high incidence rate, which lends a sense of urgency to new policies that will address the problem.

As advocates for missing children seek to expand the definition of this terrible offense to include incidents of child sexual molestation, they enter the realm of what is widely perceived as a much larger problem. Estimates of missing children almost pale in comparison to the figures advanced by the child sexual abuse prevention movement; the most frequently reported forecast is that one girl in three or four will be sexually molested before leaving high school, most often by a relative.

Unlike cases of missing children who are almost always reported to the authorities, child sexual abuse is a difficult problem to document. In 1992, an estimated 499,120 cases of child sexual abuse were reported to child protective services, approximately 40 percent were substantiated. Although an annual incidence rate of 199,648 substantiated cases (about 3 in 1000 children) represents an immense amount of suffering, it does not begin to yield a 25 to 33 percent prevalence rate over the course of childhood. However, many, if not most, incidents of child sexual abuse are never reported to the authorities. The highly publicized prevalence rates of 25 to 33 percent come from surveys of adult women, who are asked to recall if they had experienced any sexual abuse during childhood. The estimates broadcast by child sexual abuse prevention advocates reveal more about the ambiguities of this problem than its magnitude.

At least fifteen surveys conducted since 1976 have attempted to gauge the prevalence of child sexual abuse through self-reports recalled by victims. These studies estimate that the proportion of women sexually abused during their childhood ranges from 6 percent to 62 percent of the population. This is a rather wide spread with half of the studies showing a prevalence rate of 6 to 15 percent. Some of this variance can be accounted for by different research sampling procedures and data gathering techniques. But the most telling factor is the investigators' assorted working definitions of child sexual abuse.

At the high end of these estimates, one of the most extensive and most widely cited studies was conducted by Diana Russell, who reports in *Sexual Exploitation* that 54 percent of her respondents were victims of incestuous or extrafamilial sexual abuse before the age of eighteen. This prevalence rate was based on a broad definition of child sexual abuse under which children who merely receive unwanted hugs and kisses are classed as victims, as are others who have not been touched at all (for example, children who encounter exhibitionists). A lower rate of 38 percent was registered with a narrower definition that involved "unwanted sexual experiences ranging from attempted petting to rape" by persons outside the family and "any kind of exploitive sexual contact or attempted contact" by relatives. The information, used to determine an episode of sexual abuse, was based on responses to fourteen screening questions such as these:

— Did anyone ever try or succeed in touching your breasts or genitals against your wishes before you turned fourteen?
— Did anyone ever feel you, grab you, or kiss you in a way you felt was threatening?

— At any time in your life has an uncle, brother, father, grandfather, or female relative ever had any kind of sexual contact with you?

What this study characterizes as a "narrower" definition of child sexual abuse actually stretches from attempted petting to any exploitive contact such as touching on the leg or other body parts to forced sexual intercourse, fellatio, and other forms of penetration. When one thinks of child sexual abuse, an incident of attempted petting, a touch on the leg, and an unwanted pat on the buttock hardly come to mind. By lumping together relatively harmless behavior such as attempted petting with the terribly damaging ordeal of child rape, advocates have inflated the estimates of child sexual abuse to critical proportions.

More recently, in an effort to assess the effectiveness of sexual abuse prevention training programs, David Finkelhor and colleagues ("The Effectiveness of Victimization Prevention Instruction: An Evaluation of Children's Responses to Actual Threats and Assaults," 1993) report a 42 percent prevalence rate of "victimization" among 2,000 children surveyed. These "victimizations" included fights and attempted assaults by peers, gangs, or family members, kidnapping, and sexual abuse.

Measures of sexual abuse included positive responses to broadly worded questions such as: "Has there ever been a time when an older person tried to feel you, grab you, or kiss you in a sexual way that made you feel bad or afraid?"

By equating as "victimizations," school yard scraps, attempted fights, unwanted squeezes, and kisses that "feel bad" with kidnapping and rape of children, the researchers construct a 42-percent "victimization" rate, which presumably reveals the pressing need for sexual-abuse-prevention training. When sexual victimization is separated out from other forms of victimization, the prevalence rate drops to 6 percent. Since half of these involve attempted cases, the findings show an actual sexual abuse prevalence rate of 3 percent, which includes kisses and touches that felt bad.

Despite his well-intentioned advocacy of comprehensive sexual-abuse-prevention training programs, Finkelhor offers a curious interpretation of his findings to the press. In a *New York Times* (October 6, 1993) report headlined "Abuse-Prevention Efforts Aid Children," he is quoted as saying that he "finds that kids who have gotten the better sexual-abuse prevention programs do act better in the crunch." (By "better" Finkelhor is referring to the more comprehensive programs.) Yet, his data for all the cases of actual or attempted sexual victimization show no statistically significant differences on most of the major outcome variables between children who had received no or minimal prevention training and those who had participated in the most comprehensive programs.

And where there were significant differences, they were in a direction that suggested harmful outcomes of comprehensive training programs. That is, among the sexually victimized respondents, children receiving comprehensive training did not differ significantly from the others with regard to:

1) the number of preferred strategies recommended for self-protection by prevention programs which they employed during the incident; 2) their sense of efficacy in coping with their abusers; 3) their disclosures of abuse; and 4) their success in thwarting attempted abuse.

On the study's three other outcome measures, statistically significant differences revealed that when threatened with sexual abuse children who participated in comprehensive prevention training programs were more likely to fight back (a less-preferred strategy taught by one of the most widely used programs in the country), to cry, and to be physically injured. Rather than "acting better in the crunch," the firmest conclusion that can be drawn from these findings is that children with comprehensive training use less-preferred strategies and get injured more than twice as often as other children.

As the problems of child sexual abuse gained public notice, eliciting new policies and funding for prevention programs from state and federal government, advocates for the elderly discovered that children were not the only victims of maltreatment. "A National Disgrace" was the title of the 1985 report issued by the Aging Committee's Subcommittee on Health and Long-Term Care. Citing research evidence that an estimated 4 percent of the elderly or one million older citizens are victims of abuse each year, the report maintained that "abuse of the elderly by their loved ones and caretakers existed with a frequency and rate only slightly less than child abuse."

Woolly Calculations

One million victims is the kind of figure that attracts media attention. The estimated incidence rate of 4 percent gained authority merely by frequent citation. But on closer inspection the figure evaporates into a haze of woolly calculations. As Stephen Crystal explains, the estimate of one million victims is a "mythical number" based on a survey of 433 elderly residents of Washington D.C., only seventy-three of whom (16 percent of the sample) responded. Such a low response rate immediately disqualifies any generalizations drawn from the results. As it turned out, three of the seventy-three respondents, or 4.1 percent, reported experiencing some form of psychological, physical, or material abuse. By extrapolating the findings from this small and unreliable sample to show that one million elderly people are victims of abuse, advocates construct a national epidemic out of three incidents.

But keeping the number high is often only part of the agenda of advocacy research. Beyond attempts to magnify the size of their client group's problem, so that it draws public attention, advocates habitually seek to define the essential characteristics of the problem. They tend not only to see their client group's problems as approaching epidemic proportions, but are inclined to attribute the underlying causes to oppressive social conditions, such as sexism, racism, ageism, and capitalism, which can only be corrected through fundamental changes in society.

Of course, there is a relation between the size of a problem and the extent to which its cause is attributed either to social forces or to personal factors. If 4 percent of the labor force is unemployed, these workers are unskilled, unmotivated, or temporarily down on their luck; if the unemployment rate goes to 24 percent, they are victims of a depression. If 5 percent of females are sexually abused as children, the offenders are sick deviants; if 50 percent of females are sexually abused as children, the problem is "normal" male socialization to take advantage of females.

Advocacy research of homelessness has been concerned not only with inflating the estimated number of homeless, but also with defining the nature of their problem. Advocates' estimates of the number of homeless in Chicago were nine times higher than the figures produced by repeated carefully designed scientific surveys. The National Coalition of the Homeless figure of 500,000 homeless children in the United States is ten times higher than the 35,000 calculated from the Urban Institute's national sample and the 40,000 estimated by a survey conducted by the U.S. Department of Housing and Urban Development.

Advocates take these large numbers to confirm that the homeless are essentially victims of structural flaws and economic forces rather than personal deficiencies. Henry Miller, author of *On the Fringe*, concludes that the causes for the current problem "can be found in the risks attendant on the wage labor system." As he sees it, "many members of the establishment would prefer to ignore a basic structural flaw in our socioeconomic system, whose correction would require a rethinking and reconstruction of the American system, and shift the blame for homelessness to the much smaller arena of mental health and care for the mentally ill." The solution is employment. "Today's homeless," Miller explains, "need good jobs that pay decent wages. The homeless will work if they can find work."

This view of the homeless as people just like you and me who find themselves on the streets for lack of a job ignores compelling evidence to the contrary. Considerable information on this population shows that between 40 and 66 percent of homeless adults suffer from significant alcohol problems; between 33 and 50 percent of the homeless suffer from severe psychiatric disorders, such as schizophrenia; and from 10 to 25 percent of the homeless are addicted to drugs. Recognizing that alcoholism, mental illness, and drug abuse are not mutually exclusive problems, Alice Baum and Donald Burnes, in a recent issue of *Public Welfare*, estimate that 65 to 85 percent of homeless adults suffer from at least one of these disabling conditions. To avoid blaming the victim, advocates present the issue in terms of social and economic forces, which denies the essential personal problems afflicting most homeless people. Baum and Burnes' reading of the data shows that most of the homeless require above all professional treatment and humane care.

Over the last decade, problems such as abductions by strangers, child abuse, elder abuse, and homelessness have been magnified by advocacy research. But these efforts do not begin to match the remarkably powerful campaign of advocacy research inspired by the rape crisis movement in the early 1990s. This movement gained impetus from the *Ms. Magazine Campus Project on Sexual Assault* directed by Mary Koss, one of the largest, most widely disseminated and cited studies of rape on college campuses in the United States. Koss claimed that her findings showed 27 percent of college women had been victims of rape or attempted rape an average of two times between the ages of fourteen and twenty-one, and that in just the previous academic year 16.6 percent of college women were victims of rape or attempted rape, with more than half of these victims assaulted twice. Seeing rape not as an act of deviance, but as typical behavior of an average man, Koss notes that her findings support the view that sexual violence against women "rests squarely in the middle of what our culture defines as 'normal' interaction between men and women."

Rape Research

A close examination of the *Ms.* study reveals several problems: 1) almost three-quarters of the students whom Koss defined as victims of rape did not think they had been raped; 2) 42 percent of these women went back and had sex again with the men Koss says raped them; and 3) two of the five items Koss used to define incidents of rape and attempted rape were the vaguely worded questions: "Have you had a man attempt sexual intercourse when you didn't want to by giving you alcohol or drugs, but intercourse did not occur? Have you had sexual intercourse when you didn't want to because a man gave you alcohol or drugs?"

What does it mean to have sex when you don't want to "because" a man gives you alcohol or drugs? How does one attempt intercourse "by" giving you alcohol or drugs? Forty-four percent of all the women Koss identified as victims of rape and attempted rape during the previous academic year were so labeled because they responded positively to these blurry questions. Unable to explain how one might know that an affirmative response to these questions corresponds to the legal definition of rape, Koss and Cook (in a paper "Facing the Facts: Date and Acquaintance Rape") take the item as originally reported ("Have you had intercourse with a man when you didn't want to because he gave you drugs or alcohol?") and add the words "to make you cooperate."

Rather than clarifying their case, however, this revised version suggests that instead of being too drunk to deny consent, the respondent actually cooperated in the act of intercourse after taking drugs or alcohol. Later, after reviewing my comment on their attempt to clarify the case by a change of definition, Koss and Cook, in *Current Controversies on Family Violence*, deleted their explanation and concede that "for the sake of discussion it is helpful to examine what happens to the prevalence figures when these instances are removed." In this case, according to their revised estimates, the prevalence rate of rape and attempted rape declines by one-third. It is not possible to verify this new prevalence estimate from the data as reported in Koss's earlier articles. But, as noted above, calculations that can be made from the original data show that the one-year incidence rate declines by 44 percent when the item dealing with intercourse because of alcohol or drugs is removed.

It is important to examine the data that are originally reported because definitions are not the only part of the *Ms.* study that get revised when challenged. In concluding that 27 percent of the college women in her study were victims of rape (15 percent) or attempted rape (12 percent), Koss first ignores and then revises both direct responses and behavioral indicators in the research data that contradict her interpretation of the students' experiences.

Regarding the respondents direct answers to questions, not only did 73 percent of the college women classified as victims of rape disagree with Koss's interpretation of their experiences, but when these supposed victims were asked to label their experiences, findings reported by Koss and three co-authors in *Psychology of Women Quarterly* indicate that 11 percent said "they don't feel victimized," 49 percent labelled the experience "miscommunication," 14 percent labelled it "crime, but not rape;" and 27 percent said it was "rape."

When Koss's interpretation of the data was questioned three years later, she responded with four new versions of the students' responses. First, in a breathtaking disregard for the facts she originally published, she writes in the *Los Angeles Daily Journal* (July 17, 1991) that the students labeled as victims viewed the incident as follows: "One quarter thought it was rape, one quarter thought it was some kind of crime but did not believe it qualified as rape, one quarter thought it was sexual abuse but did not think it qualified as a crime, and one quarter did not feel victimized."

Second, in a later paper entitled "Rape on Campus: Facing the Facts," the gist of these new findings was revised and Koss reported: "One quarter thought it was some kind of crime, but did not realize it qualified as rape; one quarter thought it was serious sexual abuse, but did not know it qualified as a crime."

Third, Koss and Cook relate: "In fact, half the rape victims identified in the national survey considered their experience as rape or some crime similar to rape." And finally, continuing to deny that virtually one half of the students labelled their experience a case of "miscommunication," in a letter to *The Wall Street Journal* (August 3, 1993) Koss claims that "only one in ten victims said she felt unvictimized by the experience." She goes on to say, "The remaining nine who felt victimized were split between those who thought their experience was rape (the 27 percent fraction Mr. Gilbert quotes), those who thought their experience was a crime but might not be called rape, and those who thought their incident was extremely traumatic but was not a crime."

With regard to behavioral indicators, the fact that 42 percent of the purported victims had sex afterwards with their supposed assailants, would appear to support the accounts by many students that they were not raped initially. At least, this finding should raise a question about Koss's interpretation of what her survey items really meant. Indeed, when she first reported this finding in *Rape and Sexual Assault*, Koss even admitted to being somewhat baffled. "Surprisingly," she notes, "42 percent of the women indicated that they had sex again with the offender on a later occasion, but it is not known if this was forced or voluntary; most relationships (87 percent) did eventually break up subsequent to the victimization."

Three years later, after questions were raised about the *Ms.* study, Koss again revises her findings. This time, she claims in a letter to *The Wall Street Journal* (July 25, 1991) that "many victims reacted to the first rape with self-blame and thought that if they tried harder to be clear they could influence the man's behavior. Only after the second rape did they realize the problem was the man, not themselves. Afterwards, 87 percent of the women ended the relationship with the man who raped them." Following her first report in the professional literature that it was not known if sex on the later occasion was voluntary or forced, Koss now tells the public that these women were raped the second time by their purported offenders, and "afterwards," not "eventually" broke up their relationship.

It is one thing to exaggerate the extent of a problem by measuring it with broad and vaguely worded questions and then to ignore data that contradict the researcher's interpretation of these questions. But responding to a critical examination of a study by revising findings originally published to make them more compatible with the author's conclusion goes beyond what was originally a serious exaggeration of the problem to a misrepresentation of findings to the public.

Hype and Disputation

How is it that findings as flawed and inconsistent as those presented by Koss gain the confidence of the media and are lent authority by repeated acknowledgment? Initially, the findings of advocacy research often receive a favorable reception from the media. With a lack of critical scrutiny, the media at first rush to embrace the advocate's depiction of the magnitude and character of problems such as child abuse, homelessness, kidnapping, elderly abuse, and rape. There are various reasons for this willingness to suspend disbelief, having to do with journalists, their audience, and social scientists.

As documented by Robert Lichter, Stanley Rothman, and Linda Lichtman in *The Media Elite*, the majority of journalists hold distinctly liberal positions on political and social issues. This ideology often translates into concerns about victims of oppression and social ills. "Afflict the comfortable and comfort the afflicted!" the edict of a distinguished professor of journalism at Columbia University could have been the school slogan, notes Stephanie Gutmann in a recent issue of the *National Review* . The message at Columbia, she explains, was that a viable story assignment for students "could combine any three from this list: Bronx, babies, community activist, crack, homelessness, a social program that's losing its funding, single mothers, the Lower East Side, and AIDS—always AIDS." One need not attend the Columbia School of Journalism to recognize that as a rule journalists are quicker to report about experiences that are painful and sensational—kidnapping, rape, drugs, homelessness, child abuse—than those that are comfortable and ordinary. This is not only because of liberal tendencies to publicize the plight of victims. Murder and mayhem attract the public's attention for which the media compete. Advocates understand this, which is why their research data are so often accompanied by what Joel Best describes as "atrocity tales"—painfully detailed anecdotes that typify the human suffering caused by the problem, but fail to give the slightest hint of its incidence in the population.

Advocacy research benefits from the felicitous union between journalists' need to discover victims and the public's curiosity about the horrors of modern life. It also takes advantage of the journalists' general inability to evaluate data supplied to the press. Most journalists are not well-versed in social science research methods. They gather and cross-check information by interviewing experts. Since advocates are frequently among the first to uncover and publicize information about emerging problems, they are the ones who are interviewed and whose data frame the issue in the initial stages of problem discovery.

A common tactic of advocacy researchers is to declare that their estimates are well-replicated in many other studies, a claim that Koss often makes for the *Ms.* survey findings. A close look at the studies she usually cites reveals very little replication. Koss and Cook, in *Current Controversies in Family Violence*, refer to the National Victim Center study, in which 13 percent of the women surveyed were defined as victims of rape—only a few percentage points different from the 15 percent rate of rape claimed by the *Ms.* study. What Koss and Cook fail to tell the public is that approximately 40 percent of the rapes (as defined by the responses to the National Victim Center study) occurred between the ages of fourteen and twenty-four, resulting in a 5 percent rape prevalence estimate for that age group. According to the *Ms.* study, 15 percent of college women become victims of rape sometime between age fourteen and twenty-one.

Thus, for a narrower age cohort over a similar period of years, the *Ms.* study found a rate of rape three times higher than that detected by the National Victim Center survey. Several questions can also be raised about the National Victim Center survey. The definition of rape in this study includes sexual penetration by a man's fingers, which does not reflect the legal definition of rape in most states. When Nara Schoenberg and Sam Roe (*Toledo Blade*, October 10, 1993) inquired about this item, the study's director, Dean Kilpatrick, allowed that his definition "might be a tad broader" than the common legal standard. Women also were not asked directly whether they had been raped. Kilpatrick explained that there was not enough time in his thirty-five-minute telephone survey to include this question. As Schoenberg and Roe note, in an earlier survey that used more direct questions, Kilpatrick, writing in the *Journal of Consulting and Clinical Psychology*, found that one in twenty women was a victim of rape, a rate less than half that reported in his National Victims Center study.

Koss and Cook also cite Diana Russell's study, which found a rape prevalence rate of 24 percent, as offering corroborating scientific evidence from a representative sample of women. This claim disregards the fact that the participation rate in Russell's interview survey was less than 50 percent, hardly a representative sample by conventional scientific standards. It is of interest to note that Russell's findings show a lifetime prevalence rate of rape that is twice as high as that of the National Victim Center's study. At the same time, less than 1 percent of the rapes in Russell's sample were reported to have occurred when the victim was under eleven years of age whereas during the same period of life 29 percent of the rapes in the National Victim's Center sample were reported to have occurred. In light of these enormous discrepancies, the average layman as well as the social scientist must wonder what is really being measured here. To advocacy researchers like Koss and Cook, these discrepancies represent inconvenient details to be swept under the carpet of "supporting literature."

As with most of the cases Koss offers in support of her rape estimates, only by ignoring contradictory details can the results of works such as the National Victim Center's and Diana Russell's surveys be construed as independent confirmation of the *Ms.* findings. Just as the so-called supporting literature is overstated, studies that reveal relatively low lifetime prevalence rates of rape tend to receive short shrift from advocacy researchers. Linda George and her colleagues at Duke University, writing in the *Journal of Social Issues*, found a 5.9 percent lifetime prevalence rate of sexaul assault in North Carolina. This finding was based on responses to the broad question: "Has someone ever pressured you against your will into forced contact with the sexual parts of your body or their body?"

While regional differences may account for some of the disparity between the *Ms.* findings and those of the Duke University team, in 1990 the rate of rapes reported to the police in North Carolina was 83 percent of the national average. An even lower prevalence rate was detected by Margaret Gordon and Stephen Riger, who report in the *Journal of Social Issues* that among 1620 respondents, randomly selected in Chicago, San Francisco, and Philadelphia, only 2 percent had been raped or sexually assaulted in their lifetime. Gordon and Riger note, however, that among a small sub-sample of 367 respondents who were selected to be interviewed in-person and were younger, wealthier, and better educated than those in the larger random sample, 11 percent mentioned ever having been raped or sexually assaulted.

With neither the inclination nor the skill to systematically review and critically evaluate research literature, the media are easily bamboozled by claims of independent verification by other studies. Repeating Koss's claim, for example, in an article for *Newsweek* (October 25, 1993), Susan Faludi confidently asserts, "Numerous other studies bear these figures out." Among journalists, there is much fuzzy thinking and writing on this matter as reflected by Katha Pollitt's recent observations in *The New Yorker*. Disregarding serious concerns for detail and accuracy, she notes: "One in five, one in eight—what if it is only one in ten or one in twelve? Social science isn't physics. Exact numbers are important, and elusive, but surely what is significant here is that lots of different studies, with different agendas, sample populations, and methods tend in the same direction." Pollitt fails to explain, however, what "direction" she is referring to—toward one in five or one in twelve.

At the same time there are activist constituencies that lend vocal support to advocacy research claims. Newsmen seeking to verify reports about the huge incidence of rape, for example, will find many social workers and therapists in rape prevention centers and counselling programs ready to confirm the figures. These groups, of course, have a vested interest in increasing public funds to address the problem. But their support of advocacy numbers reflects more than simply an occupational stake in the problem.

Working daily with women who have suffered dreadful sexual abuses, many therapists and social workers in this field truly believe that the number of victims is as vast as professed by advocacy studies. Beyond the continuous stream of daily encounters with victims, there is some evidence that their perceptions may also be influenced disproportionately by personal experiences as victims themselves. Robin Russel and her colleagues report in the *Journal of Social Work Education* showed that graduate social work students indicated being sexually molested three times as often as students in education.

Thus, the initial absence of contradictory evidence and the presence of a well-organized constituency that will attest to their findings lend a degree of credibility to advocacy research. Although the media initially tend to promote advocacy findings, liberal tendencies and readers' curiosities aside, most journalists ultimately are interested in the truth. When new data become available or advocacy claims stretch the suspension of belief so far that someone begins to wonder where these figures really came from, the media will challenge the numbers it originally promulgated.

A 1993 *New York Times Magazine* cover story proclaimed "Rape Hype Betrays Feminism." In a critical analysis of "rape-crisis feminists," Katie Roiphe remembered a poster at college announcing that one in four women had been a victim of rape or attempted rape. "If I were really standing in the middle of an 'epidemic,' a 'crisis'—if 25 percent of my women friends were really being raped—wouldn't I know it?" she wondered. Roiphe concludes, "These posters were not presenting facts. They were advertising a mood." It was a mood, one might add, instigated by earlier stories in *The New York Times*, *Time Magazine* and in many other print media as well as television reports citing as authoritative data findings like the *Ms.* study. Roiphe's article was followed by a new round of reports on NBC television, National Public Radio, and in the press, taking a more critical look at the problem of rape on college campuses. Nara Schoenberg's and Sam Roe's three-part series, "Rape: The Making of an Epidemic," in the *Toledo Blade* article mentioned earlier, offers the most thorough and insightful coverage of this issue to date.

The data reveal why there is strong reason to doubt inflated claims of studies such as Koss's. Going beyond the exaggerated figures of advocacy researchers, Schoenberg and Roe also show that although poor and minority women are much more likely to be victims of rape than middle-class college students, their stories are seldom told and programs serving these highly vulnerable groups are underfunded compared to the vast sums spent on college campuses that average less than one rape reported annually per thousand female students.

Debunking advocacy research is almost as approved as promoting it. There are even eminent rewards for this as witnessed by the Pulitzer Prize awarded the *Denver Post* serial report debunking the estimates on missing children. In this manner, advocacy research is a thriving source of copy for the media, often providing it with two lively stories—one of hype and the other of disputation. While forming sensational headlines, the modern brand of advocacy research creates an unreliable foundation for social policy and does little to advance the credibility of social science.

5

Investigating Sexual Coercion

Del Thiessen and Robert K. Young

There is an explosion of experiments and observations reported in the literature on sexual coercion, with perhaps as many as 1,000 new studies published each year in reputable journals. In addition, a continuous flood of information and concerns is published in the public press. The experimental literature is valuable, as it offers the scientific view of sexual coercion, and reflects our attempts to understand the social and physiological mechanisms.

We analyzed the majority of scientific studies on sexual coercion published between 1982 and 1992 and classified them according to areas of interest, theoretical concerns, methodology, causal mechanisms, and attempts to manipulate behaviors. Prior to our survey, if someone had asked who investigates coercion, and what is being investigated, the answers would have been that relatively few investigations are published on sexual coercion, and published articles are empirical in nature and aimed at understanding mechanisms of rape, sexual harassment, incest and sexual abuse. We would also have suggested that male and female investigators deal with the same material and find essentially the same kinds of results.

None of our earlier beliefs was reflected in current publications, forcing us to conclude that the studies of coercion lack rigor, reflect experimenter biases, and provide almost no insights into the causal mechanisms of coercive behaviors. Male and female investigators do not tend to cooperate on publications. They look at different populations and see different things. Hardly ever is a specific hypothesis tested, a population manipulated or a statistical test employed. Populations studied and techniques applied seem to be those closest at hand, not those that can be used to answer particular questions. There are few new ideas, literally no biological investigations, and much rehashing of the themes of male oppression and female victimization.

The messages seem more political than scientific. Very few changes in emphases or results have occurred over the ten-year period, indicating an absence of scientific progress. Taken as a whole, there are few sound studies to be found in the literature, and the prospects for more objective studies are dim. These judgments are harsh, but are largely supported by the analysis of 1610 studies of sexual coercion conducted from 1982 through 1992.

The 1610 abstracts of coercion published in 443 American journals or books are available on CD Rom computer disks, containing data from the fields of psychology, educational psychology, anthropology and sociology. Among the topics covered are rape, date rape, acquaintance rape, sexual harassment, sexual abuse, and incest. Data from psychology are available on two disks, one covering 1982 to 1987, and another from 1987 to 1992. Data from educational psychology and sociology are from 1987 to 1992. The publications are highly representative of all publications on rape, sexual harassment and sexual abuse.

The populations investigated in these studies were mainly female college students between the ages of eighteen and thirty—accounting for 39.2 percent of the studies. Rape and sexual harassment studies comprised about 50 percent of the publications, with child sexual abuse and incest showing the lowest percentages. Acquaintance rape (including data rape) accounted for only 5.3 percent of the studies. Most of the investigations were focused on attitudes about rape, legal and policy considerations, and treatment of the victim. The causes of coercion, or motivations related to the behavior, were limited to 10 percent of the reports. Male and female investigators tended to study different populations. Females were more likely to study college students, women who turned to rape crises centers, children and worker populations. Males also emphasized college populations, but were more likely to investigate institutional groups, such as prisoner populations.

Empirical studies are those in which frequencies, percentages or statistics are indicated. Otherwise they are classified as non-empirical. Using this breakdown 56.5 percent of the studies were empirical and 43.2 percent were non-empirical. Empirical studies involved mainly surveys, and non-empirical studies featured mainly training and consciousness raising of female victims, aimed at giving information and comfort. The application of statistical techniques to empirical and non-empirical studies indicates that no statistics were used by investigators in the evaluation of results in about 50 percent of the studies, and probably no statistics were applied in an additional 32 percent of studies. Only 1.5 percent of the studies applied an analysis of variance statistical model, or a correlation coefficient.

The majority of empirical investigators used survey techniques. However, male and female researchers emphasized different facets in empirical as well as non-empirical investigations. Male investigators employed survey techniques much less often, and were less involved in training techniques with victims. Male investigators also tended to be less speculative and more theoretical in their conclusions. Experimental manipulations, so critical in explicating the causal mechanisms that underlie coercive behaviors, comprised a small percentages of investigations for both male and female investigators.

The majority of investigations we sampled were descriptive (48.2 percent); and hypotheses were tested in only a few cases (8.7 percent). When hypotheses were tested, 82 percent were confirmed. Regardless of the primary emphases of the studies, male and female investigators differed in their approach. Male investigators tended to team up with other males and female investigators tended to team up with females. Similar gender biases were evident in the sample studied, the subject matter of interest, and the orientation of the studies. Male investigators were likely to study males and females with equal frequency, and were slightly more likely to study rape, as opposed to other coercive behaviors. They also seemed to have less concern for the victims of coercion. Females, in contrast, were less interested in rape or the rapist, and showed greater interest in the victim.

There were virtually no changes in the nature or scope of the data collected, or the results reported, for the years 1982 to 1987 versus 1987 to 1992. In comparing early to later data, results were more "indeterminate" (22 percent as opposed to 63 percent for male authors; 22 percent as opposed to 67 percent for female authors), meaning that the outcome of recent investigations is less certain. There was also decreased emphasis on rape for both male and female authors (56 percent as against 41 percent and 56 percent as against 38 percent, respectively), reflecting a recent emphasis on studies of sexual harassment. Female authors currently express more interest in the "causes" of rape (8 percent as against 44 percent), even though "causes" are not the subject of the studies. Women seemed more apt to publish on issues of sexual coercion (41 percent as against 51 percent). Males were more likely to report survey data than they did in the past (39 percent as against 53 percent). All of these variations were statistically significant.

Our analysis of 1610 literature abstracts on sexual coercion point out many of the deficiencies in this area of study. Much of the literature, and no doubt funding, is devoted to efforts that seem highly redundant and methodologically inadequate. Our qualitative conclusion is that there has been little progress in understanding coercion during the past ten years.

Analysizing abstracts, of course, reveals only part of the story, and we may be missing some critical findings and discussions. However, abstracts correlate highly with content since investigators generally emphasize the primary methodology and findings. Inconsistency decreased as the number of abstracts increase. Our sample of 1610 studies is extensive and gives a representative picture of methods, content, and conclusions. To exhaust the range of findings, we created over 100 categories that would account for as many alternatives as possible, and we strove for consistency in scoring. A significant shortcoming of published studies is their repeated use of college students in their survey. These populations are not representative of the world at large—the amount of novel information is therefore limited. Adult non-college samples, institutionalized offenders and children among those studied least, even though they could provide new insights into coercive behaviors.

College samples are of little value in another sense. These populations are particularly sensitive to academic and political attitudes on date rape and sexual harassment, hence provide a distorted picture of the problems. Young people are constantly exposed to political views of social interactions and are encouraged to report the most minor sexual infractions as major threats. The tendency is for students to believe that all sexual advances are sexual harassment, most harassment is covert, and date rape is a non-sexual power struggle. Given these extreme points of view, the study of college samples is not likely to reveal fundamental mechanisms of coercion, or insights into how behavior can be modified. Unfortunately, surveys are used more frequently today than in the past.

There was an almost complete absence of quantification and hypothesis testing in studies of sexual coercion. Fully 40 percent of investigations dealt with victimization, consciousness raising, and treatment of the victims, whereas only 8.6 to 10 percent were directed at understanding causes. Only about 9 percent of all studies have any quantification and only 1.5 percent apply a statistical test. Experimental manipulation only occured in 5.5 percent of the cases.

This is alarming since it suggests at best a methodological indifference in this crucial area of investigation, and at worst a tendency to proselytize, speculate, and politicize. In this area, especially, an investigator can create a reputation by simply presenting extreme views. No scientific or methodological sophistication is necessary, and where it exists, it is often accused of insensitivity to social and political concerns.

Minor biases extend to the gender-linked study of populations and possible gender-driven interpretation of data. Male investigators tend to publish with each other; females do the same. Males are more likely to refer to theories, study institutionalized samples, and apply experimental manipulations. Females, by contrast, use survey instruments with college samples, are more interested in studying sexual harassment, and emphasize dealing with the victims of coercion. Finally, females tend to study females, and males tend to study males.

These differences are not an inherent bias, but they do suggest that males and females may be differentially sensitive to certain characteristics of coercive behavior, and are likely to arrive at disparate conclusions. It would be informative to look at gender patterns in published studies in other areas to see if similar differences in orientation and conclusions exist.

Two measures give an estimate of the importance of a scientific area of investigation. The first is the consistent application of strong inference, the sequential testing of alterative hypotheses, applying the Popperian strategy of falsifiability. The second measure is the inevitable progression that comes as theories are constructed and hypotheses are developed and tested. When these two criteria are applied to investigations conducted over a ten-year period, it becomes clear that no progress has been made in the area of sexual coercion. The changes that have occurred are insignificant, representing, perhaps, error of measurement. No major new findings or theoretical perspectives have appeared. Overall, scientific methods are not being applied to the understanding of sexual coercion. Consequently, we should not expect an early understanding of these complex behaviors.

There is an almost total absence of genetic, evolutionary, and physiological studies of coercion. Their numbers are too few to count; only four could be considered biological in nature (0.002 percent). Of all the approaches that might give us information on the causes of sexual coercion, these seem the most promising. Their importance has been clearly stressed by Lee Ellis and is supported by the work of Randy Thornhill and Nancy Thornhill, Martin Daly and Margo Wilson, and Robert Young and Del Thiessen. Our impression is that the bulk of the literature is indifferent or hostile to biological approaches, viewing them as antagonistic to the needs of victims. The fact that females are studied twice as frequently as males suggests that the emphasis of most studies is on dealing with the victim, rather than understanding the fundamental interactions between females and males.

The possibility exists that feminist interests enforce the orientation of published studies. Investigations of sexual coercion appear as the "cottage industry" of the feminist lobby. The work as a whole defines the female view of coercion and reflects the political perspectives of its advocates. Published studies on sexual coercion seem to have a life of their own. They change little over time or in content. They emphasize the problems of victims and place the blame on existing social policies and male oppression. There is a near-total disregard for rigorous testing of hypotheses, quantification of data and possible biological mechanisms. Many studies appear anti-scientific in conception, execution, and interpretation.

The responsibility for the proliferation of non-scientific articles and political points of view lies in part with journal editors and funding agencies. In any other academic area, this behavior would be viewed as outrageous and would not continue beyond volume one of any journal. But in the politicized arena of "women' issues," social expressions are valued beyond scientific progress. The usual high standards of major refereed journals are compromised. The authors of publications of sexual coercion serve as editors of journals and sit on grant review panels, thus creating a circle of internal support for mediocrity. Academic departments which reward these efforts must share in the blame.

The disregard for biological theories is in keeping with the overall feminist view of sexual coercion. Reference to biology is taboo, for to recognize its influence would draw the discussion toward evolutionary and genetic hypotheses of coercion, sexual dimorphism, and brain processes and would destroy the ideological fabric that cloaks the entire area of women's issues.

To counteract this trend, advocates of science should accept positions on funding agency panels and submit grant applications for studies of sexual coercion. Experimental approaches should be extended beyond survey techniques and include populations that are not usually studied. Genetic, evolutionary, and physiological studies of coercion may be extremely rewarding. Conceivably a new journal could be launched to draw together the best editorial talent and the most objective research in this area. Such a journal could be the centerpiece of a much wider scientific development.

Recommended Readings

Martin Daly and Margo Wilson. "Evolutionary Social Psychology and Family Homicide." *Science* 242 (1988): 519–24.

Lee Ellis. *Theories of Rape.* New York: Hemisphere Publishing Corporation, 1989.

Randy Thornhill and Nancy Thornhill. "Human Rape: An Evolutionary Analysis." *Ethology and Sociobiology* 4 (1983): 137–73.

6

The Myth of a "Stolen Legacy"

Mary Lefkowitz

Since its publication in 1954, *Stolen Legacy* by George G. M. James has been a bestseller among people of African descent in this country. James was an Afro-American teacher of Greek, whose other writings deal explicitly with racial issues. *Stolen Legacy* also deals with the status of black people, but in ancient rather than in modern times. The message of the book is as sensational as it is revolutionary: "The Greeks were not the authors of Greek philosophy, but the black people of North Africa, the Egyptians." This novel thesis explains "the erroneous world opinion that the African continent has made no contribution to civilization, and that its people are naturally backward; the misrepresentation that has become the basis of race prejudice, which has affected all people of color." James offers in its stead a "new philosophy of redemption for black peoples."

James's account of ancient history redirects to the black people of Africa the praise traditionally given in all Western educational institutions to the ancient Greeks: "The term Greek philosophy, to begin with, is a misnomer, for there is no such philosophy in existence." Traditional educational policy, James argues, "has led to the false worship of Socrates, Plato, and Aristotle, as intellectual gods in all the leading universities of the world." James urges black people to stop citing the Greek philosophers "because we know that their philosophy was stolen" from the black peoples of Egypt, and demands that they resign from fraternities and sororities and presumably any other institutions that honor ancient Greece. The Greeks, James insists, "did not possess the native ability essential to the development of philosophy." What is called Greek, he claims, is in fact Egyptian philosophy, plagiarized from Egyptian sources by Greeks who studied in Egypt with Egyptian priests and who learned from them the philosophy and science of the Egyptian Mystery System.

Anyone who has studied ancient Mediterranean history will realize that these assertions are untrue, both in general and in particular. Anyone who has studied the works of Plato and Aristotle, even in translation, will wonder why their instructors never referred to the Egyptian background of these philosophical works. Anyone familiar with the history of ancient philosophy will know that the "Egyptian" Mystery System James describes in his book is in fact based on an eighteenth-century French reconstruction of neoplatonic philosophy, which contains a few Egyptian elements, but is fundamentally Greek.

Anyone who has studied ancient Egyptian art is aware that the population of Egypt was racially mixed, which is to say not exclusively black at any time, though several pharaohs from Nubia and considerable cultural exchange took place with that area. To anyone unfamiliar with Egyptian or Greek history, or the works of the Greek philosophers, James's argument seems coherent and plausible, because it appears to be laid out in an informed and scholarly fashion, with copious references to ancient sources and modern historical studies. Of course, the principal reason for the success of the book is that most people who read it want to believe its thesis that an African people made the original discoveries that led to the development of what has always been known as Western thought. These readers are willing to assume that the population of ancient Egypt was black, although no evidence is presented to support this contention.

Another reason for the book's appeal is its conspiracy theory, which casts the people conspired-against in the role of innocent victims. "Had it not been for this drama of Greek philosophy and its actors, the African Continent would have had a different reputation, and would have enjoyed a status of respect among the nations of the world." If it could be shown that ancient Greeks stole or copied, without due acknowledgment, Egyptian ideas and documents, not only would the Greeks cease to be revered for their accomplishments, but credit for their great discoveries would go to the people of Egypt, an African country, and the notion that ancient African peoples produced no significant body of scientific and humanistic learning could be finally and decisively discredited.

The methods James uses to establish this erroneous and misleading thesis deserve careful study, because they have been and continue to be influential. In order to make his case as convincing as possible James does not proceed in chronological order, as is the practice in conventional histories of philosophy. Instead, he relies first of all on the tried-and-true rhetorical method of beginning with the simplest and most dramatic illustration. This he offers first in a brief summary: the Greeks began to study in Egypt when that country was occupied by the Persians, but the main transfer of information occurred after the invasion of Egypt by Alexander the Great, when Aristotle was able to take books of Egyptian philosophy and science from the library of Alexandria and convert that library into a Greek research center.

The story of Aristotle's theft is told again later in the book. Here we see how James relies on "insistence," another tried-and-true rhetorical technique. Sheer repetition served as a form of proof for the Bellman who led the expedition in Lewis Carroll's poem *The Hunting of the Snark*: "What I tell you three times is true." James insists that the Greeks had no interest in philosophy or science; they were an ambitious, envious, people who persecuted their philosophers. They were, he says, belligerent though incapable of victory over a major power like Persia. Selective use of repetition also provides a useful, if fraudulent, means of historical documentation, since the same fact can be made to support two different and mutually exclusive claims.

For example, James employs a summary of a second-century A.D. description of a contemporary initiation procession as evidence both for the education of all Egyptian priests and for the science curriculum in what he calls the higher Holy Orders. Finally, to drive his message home, James restates his main arguments once again in an appendix. But it is James' method of documentation why *Stolen Legacy* must be considered a deliberate fraud and not simply the misguided creation of an innocent or ignorant enthusiast like Lewis Carroll's Bellman.

Most of James' citations support only the unexceptionable aspects of his argument. Where exactly the works he cites apply to his discussion is never made clear, since he does not use footnotes, but only lists the sources he has consulted at the end of a section. At the beginning of his work, he mentions three books by established European scholars which "I have found helpful in my present work." But he fails to mention that none of these books supports his central thesis.

Chronology is disregarded whenever convenient, and inconsistencies and other points of view (particularly if traditional or well-established) are simply ignored. For example, in the initial chapter, James never mentions that the city of Alexandria (as its name suggests) was founded only after Alexander's conquest of Egypt, and even then remained a Greek city and was never fully integrated into the rest of the country. Neither does he mention that the library of Alexandria was built only after Aristotle's death in 322 B.C., so that he could not have sacked it, even if he had been in Egypt. James never discusses the relative reliability of ancient source materials, which can be as biased or tendentious as any modern source. He gives the same weight to late and derivative source materials as to earlier and original ones.

Silence about a "fact" is used as proof for its existence. For example, because ancient accounts of Aristotle's life say nothing about his having visited Egypt, James assumes that Aristotle and his contemporaries deliberately attempted to suppress all knowledge of his visit, so that no one would know that Egypt was the true source of his so-called original philosophy. "This silence of history at once throws doubt upon the life and achievement of Aristotle."

Once a hypothesis is laid out, it is soon treated as virtual fact, so that a remote possibility is almost immediately transformed into a distinct actuality. "Aristotle made a library of his own with plundered books, while his school occupied the building and made it a research centre." Comparisons between Egyptian and Greek texts are always made in summary rather than with explicit quotation. That way the contents can be presented so that they will seem to resemble one another more closely, and the absence of any close verbal parallels will not be noticed.

The "Egyptian Mystery System"

In order to show that Greek philosophy is stolen Egyptian philosophy James needs to establish the existence from earliest times of an "Egyptian Mystery System" which could be copied by the Greeks; that Greek philosophers studied in Egypt; and that Greek philosophers had no original ideas of their own. Although the foundation on which his thesis rests is the notion of the Egyptian Mystery System, James nowhere discusses its origins and development. He simply treats Egyptian Mysteries, temples, and schools as if their existence were an established fact. In reality, the notion of an Egyptian Mystery System is a relatively modern fiction, based on ancient sources that are distinctly Greek or Greco-Roman, and from the early Christian centuries. How this came about is too complex a story to detail here.

Suffice it to note that the earliest descriptions of academies for Egyptian priests, with large libraries and art galleries, are found not in any ancient text, but in an eighteenth-century French work of historical fiction, the novel *Séthos* by the Abbé Jean Terrasson, which was first published in 1732. Terrasson's novel was widely read; it had a profound influence on presentations of Egyptian religion, such as Mozart's *Magic Flute*. In particular, initiation of Terrasson's hero into the Egyptian priesthood served as the inspiration for Masonic rituals. It is understandable that the Masons of the eighteenth century, regarded them as both ancient and Egyptian, since their only sources about Egyptian religion were Greek and Roman and later European accounts based on them. All authentic information about early Egyptian religion was inaccessible to them, because the documents that described them could only be read after 1836 after the discovery of the Rosetta Stone and subsequent decipherment of the hieroglyphics.

James too seems to have been inspired by Masonic ritual. He speaks of Egyptian "Grand Lodges," another distinctive feature of the Masonic Order, and cites Masonic literature, such as C. H. Vail's *Ancient Mysteries and Modern Masonry* (1909), which retains the notion of Egyptian origins inspired by Terrasson, even though it was published long after it had been established that what they thought of as "Egyptian mysteries" dated not to remote Egyptian antiquity but to Greco-Roman civilization of the early Christian centuries. James's vision of the Egyptian mysteries is distinctive of African-American Masons, who claim descent from black ancient Egyptians. The Afro-American Masons believe that Masonry was founded by Africans "along the banks of the Nile."

Since Egyptian sources were not available to him, Terrasson was compelled to rely for his description of Egypt on Greek and Latin literature. For that reason, the goddess Isis assumes a particular importance in his work, as well as in works derived from it, such as Mozart's *Thamos, King of Egypt* or his *Magic Flute*. But the portrayal of Isis and her cult on which he relies is distinctively Greco-Roman. By the early Christian centuries, Isis, although in origin Egyptian, was worshipped by Greeks and Romans throughout the Mediterranean region.

The process of conversion to her cult is described in Apuleius' *The Golden Ass*, a remarkable book dating to the second century A.D. Apuleius tells the story of Lucius, a young man who travels in Greece and is turned into a jackass by a magic potion; he is rescued after many adventures by the goddess Isis, who appears to him in a dream. Lucius' conversion follows the pattern of the journey of discovery and initiation characteristic of Greek heroic myths: he undergoes physical metamorphosis; his initiation follows a period of wandering and confusion, and emerges from darkness into light. In her epiphany at the end of his journey, Isis identifies herself with many important Greco-Roman goddesses, Ceres (Demeter), Venus (Aphrodite), and Proserpina (Persephone), just to name a few. Lucius then becomes a priest of the goddess, and goes about with a shaved head like an Egyptian priest.

Because it was in the nature of Greco-Roman religion to welcome foreign gods, foreign cults, like the cult of Isis, were soon assimilated and included in the many different observances routinely followed by pious pagans. In the early third century A.D., a formal procession, similar to the rituals described by Apuleius, although basically Greek in character, could be actually be regarded as "Egyptian." This ritual James cites twice, first in describing the Egyptian priestly orders, and then as evidence of a priestly science curriculum.

Terrasson also describes a twelve-day initiation into the mysteries, but this account is primarily derived from Virgil's description in the *Aeneid* (first century B.C.) of the hero Aeneas' visit to the lower world and from Apuleius' account of his initiation to the Greco-Roman cult of Isis. The initiation culminates in a procession of priests, explicitly based on the procession described by Clement of Alexandria. Like Clement, James does not discuss the date of the ritual, but simply assumes that it was very ancient, and at least as early as the earliest Greek philosophers, some of whom date from the sixth century B.C.

In fact "mystery" or initiation cults were not established on Egyptian soil until the third century B.C. with the settlement of Alexandria after Alexander's invasion. Even then the rites were observed by Greeks living in Egypt rather than by native Egyptians. An example of such a mystery cult is the ritual of Epiphaneia at the temple of Kore in Alexandria, where after an all-night vigil the celebrants descended into a cave with torches and bring up a wooden statue. This cult is cited as an example of an "Egyptian Mystery" by the thirty-second degree Mason

Reverend Vail. But the origin of the cult is Greek, not Egyptian, and the Maiden (Kore) is Persephone, the Greek goddess of the underworld.

It is certainly understandable that Terrasson was unable to distinguish Greek from indigenous Egyptian rituals. He could not read any inscriptions or papyri that describe ancient Egyptian rites and beliefs since they were written in hieroglyphics or hieratic script, which no one at the time could read. It would also be unreasonable to suppose that the Masons, who do not pretend to be serious scholars, would have sought to revise their rituals and notions of their history in the light of the new information about Egypt that became available once it was possible to read the hieroglyphics. If James had intended to write an academic book (rather than a mythistory), he would have taken recent discoveries about Egypt into consideration.

Instead of concentrating on current knowledge about ancient Egyptian myth and ritual, James cites *Anacalypsis* (or "Revelation") by Godfrey Higgins, who died in 1833, several years before the publication of the definitive version of Jean François Champollion's decipherment of hieroglyphics. Higgins argues vigorously against the Champollion's and Thomas Young's preliminary studies of hieroglyphics (which later proved to be correct), claiming that the Rosetta Stone, on which Champollion's decipherment was based, was a forgery. He was, of course, completely wrong. That James should cite Higgins rather than a more authoritative, modern source suggests that he was more interested in presenting a particular viewpoint than getting at the truth.

Higgins argued that Egyptian writing could never be deciphered because it was a "secret" system. In *Stolen Legacy* James likewise insists that no records (in any language) of the Egyptian Mystery System have come down to us because it was secret. James does not mention the other, and more obvious, explanation for the absence of records, which is, of course, that no such system ever existed. The rituals identified by writers of late antiquity as Egyptian are basically Greek. These ersatz-Egyptian rituals are the models for the impressive "Egyptian" rituals described by Terrasson, which directly, and indirectly, served as inspiration for the Masons.

Thus most ironically, the "Egyptian Mystery System" described by James is not African, but essentially Greek, and in its details, specifically European. James has in effect accused the Greeks of borrowing from themselves and has said nothing about the real distinctively Egyptian ideas that influenced the Greeks during the long contact between the two peoples. The best evidence for the interchange of ideas between Greece and Egypt comes from the period after Alexander's conquest when Egypt was ruled by the Ptolemaic dynasty.

We can derive from these later sources appreciative accounts of the character of Egyptian religion and the learning and asceticism of its priests. The first-century-A.D. temple scribe and Stoic philosopher Chaeremon, who wrote in Greek, found among the Egyptian priests the Stoic ideal of the wise man. He describes their piety and knowledge of astronomy, arithmetic and geometry, recorded in sacred books. The Christian writer Clement of Alexandria preserved a description of a procession of Egyptian priests carrying forty-two treatises containing what he calls "all of Egyptian philosophy." The subject matter of these treatises included hymns, astrology, cosmography, temple construction and provisions, sacrifice, priestly training, and various branches of medicine.

James describes this procession twice, first as the description of the Egyptian priestly orders, and then as evidence for the priestly science curriculum. Here is undoubtedly one source of James' notion that there was a corpus of Egyptian philosophy. Even if we ignore the problem of chronology and assume that the works Clements lists in the second century A.D. are copies of traditional ancient writings, it is important to note that by "philosophy" Clement meant not what we now call philosophy, but learning in general, and in this particular case a body of knowledge that had little or no connection with anything Greek.

Another possible source of the notion that Greek philosophy derived from Egyptian thought comes from the Egyptians themselves, but only in the early Christian centuries, hundreds of years after the Plato's and Aristotle's death. These writings purport to have been composed at the beginning of time by Hermes Trismegistus, grandson of the god, but in fact they are much influenced by later thought, including Plato, Aristotle, and their followers, and the Hebrew writers known as Gnostics.

The writer of one of these treatises has the god Asclepius complain of the difficulty of translating Egyptian, which is direct and onomatopoeic, into the excess verbiage of Greek. There apparently was no Egyptian-language original from which they were derived and in fact they could not have been composed without the conceptual vocabulary and rhetoric of Greek philosophy.

There is, finally, a third source of the notion that the Greeks learned from the Egyptians rather than vice versa, and that is the ancient Greeks themselves. Greeks, from Herodotus on, who were impressed by the piety and learning of the Egyptian priesthood, and reported that their leading philosophers studied in Egypt, among them the legendary Thales and Pythagoras in the sixth century B.C., then in the fourth century B.C. Plato and Eudoxus. James, of course, is very impressed by this "evidence," but from the point of view of history, it is important to note that the fullest account of the visits of Greek philosophers to Egypt is given by Diodorus of Sicily, a Greek writer of the first century B.C.

Greek Philosophers in Egypt?

Diodorus says that the Egyptian priests of his day relate that various Greek poets and philosophers visited Egypt. He cites as evidence statues, houses, and inscriptions with their names, and illustrates what each of them admired and transferred from Egypt to their own country. It is clear from Diodorus' account that the term "philosopher" applied to a considerably less specialized class of individuals in his day than it has become in ours. In the ancient world holy men, poets, prophets, mathematicians, and theoretical logicians were all lumped together under the general rubric of philosopher.

The similarities that are cited by the priests are superficial at best and do not stand up to close examination. For example, the priests observed that the mysteries of Demeter and Persephone were "similar" to the rite of Osiris and Isis, except for a difference in names in each case. But while it is certainly true that the myths connected with both cults involve a goddess' search for a missing relative, there are also many significant differences in detail and outcome which suggest that the myths, despite this one similarity, have no direct connection at all. Similarly, the priests pointed out that both Egyptian and Greek myths tell of a dwelling place of the dead located beyond a body of water. Here Egyptian notions may have had some influence on early Greek myth, but their beliefs about the fate of the soul after death and their burial customs diverge widely.

It is clear from these and other instances cited by the priests that they were determined to make the most of any and all resemblances between the religious observances of two cultures. But since they had no information about religious rites as they had been practiced at the time of Pythagoras' or Plato's visit to Egypt, they were compelled to make their deductions on the basis of the rituals practiced in their own times, after several centuries of Greek occupation and influence. They point out that the Egyptians, like the Greeks, call the ferryman of the dead "Charon" without realizing that the Egyptians got the name from the Greeks in the first place. Like Clement of Alexandria in his description of the procession of Isis, the priests in their enthusiasm to establish the primacy of Egyptian culture fell into the trap of citing as evidence of Egyptian influence on Greek custom what was clearly Greek influence on Egyptian.

The Egyptian priests in Diodorus' account are even less explicit about the Egyptian influence on what we now call philosophy. They claim that Lycurgus, Plato, and Solon "transferred many instances of Egyptian practices into their law codes," but cite no examples. In fact the only recognizable similarities are that both Egyptians and Greeks had laws. On that basis it would be possible to conclude that any earlier civilization "influenced" any later civilization, even if they had little or no opportunity for contact with one another. Using this same methodology, Jews living in Alexandria in the second and first centuries B.C. could claim that Plato studied with Moses.

There are also significant problems with some of the other claims made by the priests about what Greek philosophers learned in Egypt. According to the priests, Pythagoras took from Egypt his teachings about religion, geometry, number theory, and the transmigration of souls. Although we know that the Greeks based their mathematical theories on the arithmetical calculations of both Babylonians and Egyptians, there is in fact nothing in Egyptian religion that resembles Pythagoras' theory of the transmigration of souls. If he had to get it from some other religion, and did not simply invent it himself, it would have had to come from India. The priests also claim that Democritus, Oenopides, and Eudoxus studied astrology in Egypt. But here again the priests seem not to have been aware that astrology was primarily a Greek invention, brought to Egypt after the conquest of Alexander. The Greeks could have learned about astronomy from the builders of the pyramids, but on that subject the priests were silent.

Although Diodorus' account of the Greek philosophers' visits to Egypt tells us virtually nothing about Egyptian philosophy and makes no convincing claims about the dependence of Greek culture on the Egyptian, it does show how eager the Egyptians were to establish such connections, and how willing Greeks like Diodorus were to believe them. For example, the fourth-century-A.D. pagan writer Iamblichus says that Pythagoras and Plato read the writings of Hermes on old stone tablets in hieroglyphics; but, of course, we know that these treatises were written in Greek centuries after the death of these philosophers and are themselves dependent upon Plato.

Even in the fifth century B.C. the Greeks had a profound respect for the antiquity of Egyptian culture. Herodotus was very keen to make any connections and tried to match up the Greek gods with their Egyptian counterparts. He even went so far as to claim that the names of the Greek gods came from Egypt, but the few examples he produced do not stand up to modern linguistic analysis. He pointed out that Greek myth suggests that parts of Greece were colonized by Egyptians, or at least by Egyptians descended from Greeks who had emigrated there. But such vague and imaginative correspondences, even if they could be confirmed by archaeological discoveries, do not amount to any kind of proof that Greek philosophy was "stolen" from Egypt. Whatever the Greek philosophers and holy men learned in Egypt, if indeed all of them went there, it was not what we call "philosophy."

Since ancient biographers relied on the works of ancient writers as their prime source material, their information is only as reliable as the author himself. In other words, if an ancient author says nothing about his travels or personal life, the information in his biography has been deduced and inferred from his works. And since the works of most of the philosophers mentioned by Diodorus survive only in fragments, it is impossible to know whether the biographical information that we have is based on what they themselves said or on what later writers thought they might have done on the basis of their writings. Foreign travel in particular was used by biographers as a means of explaining why writers included references to foreign customs and geography in their works.

Did the great philosophers whose works still survive ever go to Egypt? None of the accounts of the lives of Socrates or Aristotle says anything about their travels there. Socrates is in fact recorded by a close contemporary, Plato, as saying that during his lifetime he never went outside of Athens unless he was on a military campaign—which would have kept him in Greece. Although Plutarch, in the second century A.D., as did other late biographers, claims that Plato himself studied in Egypt, and even name his teachers, it is worth noting that the earliest biographical information we have about him says nothing about it. Since Plato's writings show some knowledge of Egyptian customs, religion, and legends, or at least of Greek ideas about Egypt, most classical scholars believe that the story of his sojourn in Egypt was invented by later biographers to explain his interest in Egypt, and to provide physical "proof" of the importance of Egyptian culture that (as we have seen) the Egyptian priests in later antiquity were eager to establish.

James argues that silence about a sojourn in Egypt by Socrates and Aristotle is proof of a conspiracy to conceal from posterity the extent of the Greeks' debt to Egypt. Presumably the same argument could be made about the failure of Plato's earliest biographer to speak about his travels there. But, of course, the same evidence of silence has led other scholars to the natural conclusion that none of them actually ever went there. If the great Greek philosophers had stolen their ideas from the Egyptians, as James asserts, we would expect James to provide corresponding texts showing frequent verbal parallels. As it is, he can only point to some general similarities between Egyptian religious ideas and Greek theories.

As James observes, Aristotle wrote a treatise *On the Soul*; the Egyptians believed in the immortality of the soul. But there the similarity ends. James admits that there is no close resemblance, because Aristotle's theory is only a "very small portion" of the Egyptian "philosophy" of the soul, as described in the Egyptian *Book of the Dead*. Anyone who looks at a translation of the *Book of the Dead* can see that it is not a philosophical treatise, but a series of ritual prescriptions that will ensure the soul's passage to the next world. Nothing could be farther removed from Aristotle's abstract consideration of the nature of the soul.

Many more examples of James's fraudulent claims could be produced. For example he insists that the Greeks did not win the war against Persia in 490 and 480/79 B.C. and claims, without evidence of any kind, that the battles of Marathon and Salamis had been indecisive. James misrepresents history to depict the ancient Greeks as quarrelsome and chaotic, incapable of producing philosophy, which (according to James) "requires an environment which is free from disturbance and worries." Such misinformation entitles *Stolen Legacy* to a place on the shelf of hate literature next to such works as *The Secret Relationship Between Blacks and Jews*.

It is, of course, possible to sympathize with James and his anger at a society that has paid little tribute to real African achievements. The trouble is that *Stolen Legacy* has been treated not as mythistory but as a serious work of scholarship.

As such it has had a wide and pernicious influence. One of James's best-known pupils, Yosef A. A. ben-Jochannan, has lectured at universities throughout the United States about the Greeks' theft of indigenous African culture and has added new details and references that make the story sound more credible. In his book *Africa: Mother of Western Civilization* (1971, reprinted 1988) ben-Jochannan claims not only that Aristotle was educated in Egypt, stole entire libraries there from the Egyptian Mysteries System, but that he either put his own name on the works he had stolen or sent them to his friends. Books he did not like or understand, he had destroyed.

According to ben-Jochannan, such "revelations" are examples of the academic dishonesty of educators who attribute Aristotle's philosophy to Greek origins. Thus when classicists or Egyptologists point out where James was wrong, they are accused of Eurocentrism and even "white racism." Such charges, even without foundation, can be damaging in today's academic world. I have been accused of both for saying that the historical evidence that has come down to us simply does not support the notion that the Greeks "stole" their civilization or their philosophy from Egypt. Although I have the greatest respect for ancient Egypt and its civilization, the ancient Greeks deserve full credit for their own achievements.

7

On Self-Suppression

James S. Coleman

There are taboos on certain topics, taboos which if broken lead to sanctions not primarily from administrators or the general public, but from one's own colleagues. (It was not always so. The research and writing of professors were once far more subject to the norms of the larger community than they are today. At the University of Chicago, for example, a distinguished sociologist, W. I. Thomas, was spied upon, harassed, and finally driven out of the university by a newspaper whose publisher regarded Thomas's research on prostitution to be a violation of community mores.)

The taboos that a sociologist is most likely to encounter are those concerning questions of differences between genders or differences between races that might be genetic in origin. Any research on the social factors leading to homosexuality that begins with the premise that homosexuality is less natural than heterosexuality would be under a similar taboo. And there are other topics with taboos less strong. What interests and concerns me is the defining characteristic of these taboos, and how they are held in place. For it is these taboos on the raising of certain questions, the gentleman's agreement that certain questions remain unexamined, that constitute one major threat to academic freedom in universities and colleges. What is more, it is a threat that operates not merely through pressures from colleagues, but also through self-suppression. It is this phenomenon of self-suppression that I want to focus on today.

I will do so by recounting an incident, one I had long put out of mind until I was reminded of it recently by a research proposal of one of my students, a Hispanic student of the sociology of education. In the proposal, a well-designed study of the interaction between elementary school students and teachers, my student pointed out that there is a large and increasing disparity between the proportion of minority students and the proportion of minority teachers. The student raised the question (often raised concerning black students with white teachers, but here concerning Hispanic students with non-Hispanic teachers) of whether the cultural difference might contribute to the educational disadvantage experienced by Hispanic students in American schools. This is a reasonable question, but it reminded me of another I once failed to ask in research on inequality of educational opportunity.

The occasion was this: In 1965–66, under a provision of the Civil Rights Act of 1964, the United States Office of Education (as it was then called) was carrying out a survey of the lack of equality of education by race, and I was directing the study, on part-time loan from Johns Hopkins University. The research arrived at some results we had not expected, of which three were most important. First, we discovered that the facilities and resources of schools attended by black and white children in the same region and urban-rural settings differed very little; the principal differences in resources and facilities were between regions and rural-urban settings, not between races within these settings. This did lead to inequalities of resources and facilities by race, but only through their different distributions across the country.

Second, we found that even if the resource distribution had been different it would not have mattered very much: differential effectiveness of different schools was not closely related to the resources put into the schools by school boards, nor to per pupil expenditure, age of textbooks, or a host of other measures of presumed school quality. To understand how this second result could be so, how the outputs of education could be unrelated to the school inputs, it is only necessary to shift the context. In the industries of Eastern Europe and the Soviet Union, which, like American public schools, operate under state management free from the market discipline created by consumer choice, outputs also have very little relation to inputs. In such systems, the forces that would bring this about are largely missing.

On the other hand, there was one school resource that we did find more highly related to student achievement than others. Teachers were given a short vocabulary test in the survey, and we found that the teachers' scores on vocabulary tests were related to the verbal achievement of students in the school. Other characteristics of teachers were not, including degrees, experience, and salary; but vocabulary test score was related.

The third result of the research was that black children achieved more highly in schools with student bodies that were predominantly middle-class. Although the official school resources mattered little for their achievement, the resources provided by what fellow students brought to school did make a difference—not as much as their own family back-grounds, but more than the school board's resources.

These results had various consequences. The first two were strongly opposed within the Department of Health, Education, and Welfare, for they went against conventional wisdom as well as the recently initiated federal policy of funding school physical facilities. The third result was used by plaintiffs in school desegregation cases, including the city-wide busing cases that were initiated over the next several years. But there is one result about which little was said. It is the result to which I now want to return: the relation of teachers' vocabulary scores to student achievement. One of the policy issues that was current at the time, a necessary accompaniment of school desegregation, was the future of black teachers as the formerly segregated school systems of the South were dismantled. These teachers were at a disadvantage because of the strong prejudice held by many Southern whites against having their children taught by black teachers. But they were also at another disadvantage: themselves products of segregated school systems, they were on the whole less prepared and qualified, with lower verbal skills than their white counterparts.

What does this mean for the research? The question we did not ask was one directly connected to our research finding that children's verbal achievement in school was related to the vocabulary test scores of the teachers in the school. This finding, taken together with the fact that black teachers were generally not as well-prepared as white teachers leads immediately to a question directly relevant to the policy issue of the fate of black teachers from formerly segregated school systems: How is the achievement of black children related to the racial composition of the teaching staff in the school?

These two facts would also lead to the conjecture that black children would be doing less well, on average, under black teachers than under white teachers. In contrast, the role-modeling or cultural difference hypothesis that is implicit in my Hispanic student's research proposal would lead to the opposite conjecture, that they would be doing better, on average, under black teachers. But if the first conjecture were right, it would have some disturbing implications. One would be that a major source of inequality of educational opportunity for black students was the fact that they were being taught by black teachers. Another, directly relevant to the policy issue, would be that both black and white children would have greater educational opportunity if they were not taught by these teachers. It is this potential implication, I suggest, that was the cause of our not asking the research question that followed from the results we had found.

Perhaps it was not this. We had many other things to keep us busy, many other battles to fight with agency officials who did not like our results, many problems in merely maintaining the integrity of the research report in the face of attempts to rewrite or to undermine it altogether. Yet I believe that a dispassionate researcher concerned with finding facts relevant to the policy issues at hand (one of which was school staff desegregation) would have gone on to pose the question we did not ask. One could well argue that by not asking it, we aided in the sacrifice of educational opportunity for many children, most of whom were black, to protect the careers of black teachers. And one could argue that by not asking it, we encouraged the continued neglect of the kind of skill-specific retraining programs—not only for black teachers, but for all teachers— that might have brought improvements in educational outcomes.

But my principal concern here is not this policy issue. It is, rather, about the source of the self-suppression of a research question, the impulse not to ask the crucial question—an impulse, if I am correct, that prevents many relevant research questions from being raised. These questions are not generally of the kind that are clearly taboo among university researchers, yet they are nonetheless subject to more subtle pressures leading to the self-suppression of research.

How do these subtle pressures arise? I believe it can be put this way. We hesitate to ask research questions which might lead to results that would elicit disapproval by those colleagues we see regularly. We monitor our own activities, and suppress those that do not meet this criterion. When there is a strong consensus among these colleagues, we redirect our behavior accordingly. The stakes are not trivial. I think of a sociologist who, during the fervor of the 1960s, asked the wrong questions and came out with answers inimical to the school desegregation policies favored by his fellow sociologists, and subsequently failed to get tenure. I know also from personal experience on similar occasions the strength of such attacks.

What are the kinds of results that most strongly elicit disapproval by one's colleagues in universities? The answer is not always and everywhere the same, but I believe that for many academics in many settings, the following can be said: There are certain policies, certain public activities, that have the property that they stem from benevolent intentions expressed toward those less fortunate or in some way oppressed. The intended consequences follow transparently from the policy. These are policies designed to aid the poor, or to aid blacks or Hispanics or women, and any result that would hinder one of these policies is subject to disapproval and attack. These are policies intended to display egalitarian intentions. For many academics they replace the patterns of conspicuous consumption that Thorstein Veblen attributed to the rich. They might be called policies of conspicuous benevolence. They display, conspicuously, the benevolent intentions of their supporters.

The consensus about such policies among academics stems, if I am not mistaken, from a general view that there is a single broad conflict in public policy and political affairs between those with good intentions, who want to help the disadvantaged, and those who are selfish and opposed to any aid to those less fortunate. This view manifests itself in a thousand ways. It was the source of widespread support for communism among intellectuals in the 1920s and 1930s. It is the source of widespread support for sanctions against South Africa today, for civil rights measures, for school busing policies, for generous welfare provisions, for bills to aid the handicapped, for the Equal Rights Amendment. Sometimes the support is well-placed. Sometimes it is not.

The conflict between this conspicuous benevolence and dispassionate research on the consequences of social policy lies in the difference between intentions and consequences. A former teacher of mine, Robert K. Merton, has pointed out that because the indirect consequences of social action may be very different from its intended consequences, much of sociology consists of examining the unintended consequences of purposive action.[1] The policies of conspicuous benevolence are not, unfortunately, immune to this principle that intentions do not equal consequences, and may in fact harm just what they are intended to help. But so long as there is a consensus among academics on the policies of conspicuous benevolence, self-suppression will prevent their serious questioning.

How may that consensus be opposed or undone? The problem is a fundamental one, because a university is a community, and a department is a community within that community. It is within such communities that norms grow and thrive. A norm about what is the "correct" thing to teach and what is the "correct" research to carry out constitutes an assumption by the community of the right to disapprove or otherwise sanction a member on the basis of his research or teaching. Members of that community feel an obligation—one that sometimes leads to the self-suppression I have described earlier—to accede to such community rights. In a different context Sidney Hook wrote about this, recognizing the close connection between community and rights accompanied by obligation. In the first of his lectures published as *The Paradoxes of Freedom*, he says,

> obligation is derived from the reflective judgment that some shared goal, purpose, need—some shared interest, want, or feeling—requires the functioning presence of these rights. Without some common nature or some community of feeling, the sense of obligation could hardly develop: the assertion of rights would have no binding or driving emotional force.[2]

As Sidney Hook wrote, community generates rights, rights generate obligation—and it is this obligation that leads, in the case under question, to the self-suppression of academic freedom.

Yet there is a way out. There are hierarchies of shared values in a community, and therefore hierarchies of rights. If, in the hierarchy of values held by the academic community of which one is a part, the value of freedom of inquiry is higher than the value of equality (the value that gives rise to conspicuous benevolence), then such constraints, such self-suppression of research into inconvenient questions, will no longer be effective. It is this, I submit, which is lacking in many university settings. If it were present, the community of which Sidney Hook wrote, and the sense of obligation it entailed, would lead to the pursuit of inconvenient questions without constraint.

In the absence of such a hierarchy of values, with freedom of inquiry above equality, the most efficacious means to insure that inconvenient questions are pursued may lie in the creation of a community within the university that can insulate its members from the effects of the general pressure toward conspicuous benevolence. The creation of such a community cutting across universities, an "invisible college" spanning the academic community as a whole, may constitute another means. In this second alternative lies the importance of the insulation provided by an association like the National Association of Scholars. Were Sidney Hook here today, he would be pleased with the activities that carry on his fight for academic freedom.

Notes

1. Robert K. Merton, *Social Theory and Social Structure* (New York: Free Press, 1949), 51
2. Sidney Hook, *The Paradoxes of Freedom* (Berkeley: University of California Press, 1962), 4.

8

The Egalitarian Fiction

Linda S. Gottfredson

Social science today condones and perpetuates a great falsehood—
one that undergirds much current social policy. This falsehood, or "egalitarian fiction," holds that racial-ethnic groups never differ in average
developed intelligence (or, in technical terms, g, the general mental ability
factor). While scientists have not yet determined their source, the existence of sometimes large group differences in intelligence is as well-
established as any fact in the social sciences. How and why then is this
falsehood perpetrated on the public? What part do social scientists themselves play, deliberately or inadvertently, in creating and maintaining it?
Are some of them involved in what might be termed "collective fraud?"

Intellectual dishonesty among scientists and scholars is, of course,
nothing new. But watchdogs of scientific integrity have traditionally
focused on dishonesty of individual scientists, while giving little attention to the ways in which collectivities of scientists, each knowingly
shaving or shading the truth in small but similar ways, have perpetuated
frauds on the scientific community and the public at large.

Perhaps none of the individuals involved in the egalitarian fiction
could be accused of fraud in the usual sense of the term. Indeed, I would
be the first to say that, like other scientists, most of these scholars are
generally honest. Yet, their seemingly minor distortions, untruths, eva-
sions, and biases collectively produce and maintain a witting falsehood.
Accordingly, my concern here is to explore the social process by which
many otherwise honest scholars facilitate, or feel compelled to endorse,
a scientific lie.

The Egalitarian Fiction

It is impossible here to review the voluminous evidence showing that racial-ethnic differences in intelligence are the rule rather than the exception (some groups performing better than whites and others worse), and that the well-documented black-white gap is especially striking. All groups span the continuum of intelligence, but some groups contain greater proportions of individuals that are either gifted or dull than others.

Three facts regarding these group differences are of particular importance here for together they contradict the claim that there are no meaningful group differences.

1) Racial-ethnic differences in intelligence are real. The large average group differences in mental test scores in the United States do not result from test bias, which is minuscule overall, as even a National Academy of Science panel concluded in 1982. Moreover, intelligence and aptitude tests measure general mental abilities, such as reasoning and problem solving, not merely accumulated bits of knowledge—and thus tap what experts and laymen alike view as "intelligence."

2) Regardless of how we choose to construe them, differences in intelligence are of great practical importance. Overall they predict performance in school and on the job better than any other single attribute or condition we have been able to measure. Intelligence certainly is not the only factor that affects performance, but higher levels of intelligence greatly increase people's odds of success in many life settings.

3) Group disparities in intelligence are stubborn. Although individuals fluctuate somewhat in intelligence during their lives, differences among groups seem quite stable. The average black-white difference, for example, which appears by age six, has remained at about 18 Stanford-Binet IQ points since it was first measured in large national samples over seventy years ago. It is not clear yet why the disparities among groups are so stubborn—the reasons could be environmental, genetic, or a combination of both—but so far they have resisted attempts to narrow them. Although these facts may seem surprising, most experts on intelligence believe them to be true but few will acknowledge their truth publicly.

Misrepresentation of Expert Opinion

The 1988 book *The IQ Controversy: The Media and Public Policy* by psychologist-lawyer Mark Snyderman and political scientist Stanley

Rothman provides strong evidence that the general public receives a highly distorted view of opinion among "IQ experts." In essence, say Snyderman and Rothman, accounts in major national newspapers, newsmagazines, and television reports have painted a portrait of expert opinion that leaves the impression that "the majority of experts in the field believe it is impossible to adequately define intelligence, that intelligence tests do not measure anything that is relevant to life performance, and that they are biased against minorities, primarily blacks and Hispanics, as well as against the poor."

However, say the authors, the survey of experts revealed quite the opposite:

> On the whole, scholars with any expertise in the area of intelligence and intelligence testing...share a common view of [what constitute] the most important components of intelligence, and are convinced that [intelligence] can be measured with some degree of accuracy. An overwhelming majority also believe that individual genetic inheritance contributes to variations in IQ within the white community, and a smaller majority express the same view about the black-white and SES [socioeconomic] differences in IQ.

Unfortunately, such wholesale misrepresentation of expert opinion is not limited to the field of intelligence, as Rothman has shown in parallel studies of other policy-related fields such as nuclear energy or environmental cancer research. However, the study of IQ experts revealed something quite surprising. Most experts' private opinions mirrored the conclusions of psychologist Arthur Jensen, whom the media have consistently painted as extreme and marginal for holding precisely those views.

As Snyderman and Rothman point out, the experts disclosed their agreement with this "controversial" and putatively marginal position only under cover of anonymity. No one, not even Jensen himself, had any inkling that his views now defined the mainstream of expert belief. Although Jensen regularly received private expressions of agreement, he and others had been, as Snyderman and Rothman note, widely castigated by the expert community for expressing some of those views. Several decades ago, most experts, among them even Jensen, believed many of the views that the media now wrongly describe as mainstream—for example, that cultural bias accounts for the large black-white differences in mental test scores.

While the private consensus among IQ experts has shifted to meet Jensen's "controversial" views, the public impression of their views has not moved at all. Indeed, the now-refuted claim that tests are hopelessly biased is treated as a truism in public life today. The shift in private, if not public, beliefs among IQ experts is undoubtedly a response to the overwhelming weight of evidence which has accumulated in recent decades on the reality and practical importance of racial-ethnic differences in intelligence. This shift is by all indications a begrudging one, and certainly no flight into "racism."

Snyderman and Rothman found that as many IQ experts as journalists and science editors (two out of three) agreed with the statement that "strong affirmative action measures should be used in hiring to assure black representation." Fully 63 percent of the IQ experts described themselves as liberal politically, 17 percent as middle of the road, and 20 percent as conservative—not much different than the results for journalists (respectively, 64, 21, and 16 percent).

Moreover, as Snyderman and Rothman suggest (and as is consistent with personal accounts by Jensen and others), many of the surveyed experts, while agreeing with Jensen's conclusions, may disapprove of his expressing these conclusions openly. Consistent with this, when queried about their respect for the work of fourteen individuals who have written about intelligence or intelligence testing, the IQ experts rated Jensen only above the widely (but apparently unjustly) vilified Cyril Burt.

Despite the fact that most agreed with Jensen, they rated him far lower than often like-minded psychometricians who had generally stayed clear of the fray. Jensen even received significantly lower ratings than his vocal critics, such as psychologist Leon Kamin, whose scientific views are marginal by the experts' own conclusions. By contrast, the experts in environmental cancer research behaved as one would expect; they gave higher reputational ratings to peers who are closer to the mainstream than to high-profile critics. Snyderman's and Rothman's findings therefore suggest that a high proportion of experts are misrepresenting their beliefs or are keeping silent in the face of a public falsehood. It is no wonder that the public remains misinformed on this issue.

Living Within a Lie

IQ experts feel enormous pressure to "live within a lie," to use a phrase by Czech writer and leader Vaclav Havel characterizing daily life under communist rule in Eastern Europe. Havel argued, in *The Power of the Powerless*, that, by living a lie, ordinary citizens were complicit in their own tyranny. Every greengrocer, every clerk who agreed to display official slogans not reflecting his own beliefs, or who voted in elections known to be farcical, or who feigned agreement at political meetings, normalized falsification and tightened the regime's grip on thought. Each individual who lived the lie, who capitulated to "ideological pseudo-reality," became a petty instrument of the regime.

As many commentators have noted, Americans may not speak certain truths about racial matters today. To adapt a phrase, there is a "structured silence." Social scientists had already begun subordinating scientific norms to political preferences and creating much of our current pseudo-reality on race by the mid-1960s. Sociologist Eleanor Wolf, in a 1972 article in Race, for example, detailed her distress at how fellow social scientists were misusing research data to support particular positions on civil rights policy: presenting inconclusive data as if it were decisive; lacking candor about "touchy" subjects (such as the undesirable behavior of lower-class students); blurring or shaping definitions (segregation, discrimination, racism) to suit "propagandistic" purposes; making exaggerated claims about the success of favored policies (compensatory education and school integration) while minimizing or ignoring contrary evidence. As a result, social science and social policy are now dominated by the theory that discrimination accounts for all racial disparities in achievements and well-being.

This theory collapses, however, if deprived of the egalitarian fiction, as does the credibility of much current social policy. Neither could survive intact if their central premise were scrutinized. No wonder, then, that IQ researchers find themselves under great professional and institutional pressure to avoid not only engaging in such scrutiny but even appearing to countenance it. The scrutiny itself must be discredited; the egalitarian fiction must be raised above serious scientific question. Scientists must at least appear to believe the dogma. As was the case in Havel's communist-dominated Eastern Europe, in American academe feigned belief in the official version of reality is maintained largely by routine obeisance of academics as they pursue their own ambitions.

Scholars realize their scholarly ambitions primarily through other scholars. Peer recognition is the currency of academic and scientific life. It is crucial to a scholarly reputation and all the steps toward status and success—publications, professional invitations and awards, promotion, tenure, grants, fellowships, election to professional office, appointment to prestigious panels. One's ability even to carry out certain kinds of research, funded or not, may be contingent upon peer recognition and respect—for instance, getting collaborators, subjects, or cooperation from potential research sites. Just as in personal life, a high professional reputation depends upon a sustained history of "appropriate" behavior, and it may be irreparably damaged by hints of scandal or impropriety.

Similarly, the reputations of scientists and their organizations are enhanced or degraded by those for whom they show regard and approval. Associating oneself with highly regarded individuals or ideas enhances, even if slightly, one's own status. Awarding an honor to a luminary can enhance the reputation of one's own organization, especially if the recipient accepts the honor with genuine appreciation. By the same token, one risks "staining" one's reputation by associating with, honoring, defending, or even failing to condemn the "wrong" sort of individual or idea. In short, how one gives or withholds one's regard is important for one's professional reputation because it affects the regard one receives.

Such a social system enhances the integrity of science and is furthered by personal ambition when the members of the community base their regard on scholarly norms, such as competence, creativity, and intellectual rigor. However, such a system breeds intellectual corruption when members systematically subordinate scientific norms to other considerations—money, politics, religion, fear.

This is what appears to be happening today in the social sciences on matters of race and intelligence. As sociologist Robert Gordon argues, social science has become "one-party science." Democrat or Republican, liberal or conservative, virtually all American intellectuals publicly adhere to, if not espouse, the egalitarian fiction. And many demonstrate their party loyalty by enforcing the fiction in myriad small ways in their academic routine, say, by off-handedly dismissing racial differences in intelligence as "a racist claim, of course," criticizing authors for "blaming the victim," or discouraging students and colleagues from doing "sensitive" research. One can feel the gradient of collective alarm and disapproval like a deepening chill as one approaches the forbidden area.

Researchers who cross the line occasionally face overt censorship, or calls for it. For example, one prominent (neoconservative) editor rejected an author's paper, despite finding it scientifically sound, because there are social "considerations" which "overweigh the claims of social science." Another eminent editor, after asking an author to soften the discussion in his article, recently published the revised paper with an editorial postscript admonishing scientists in the field to find a "balance" between the need for free exchange of research results on intelligence and the (presumably comparable) "need" that "no segment of our society...feel threatened" by it.

Covert and Overt Censorship

Whether motivated by a sincere concern over supposedly "dangerous" ideas or by a desire to distance themselves publicly from unpopular ideas, editors who use such non-academic standards discourage candor and stifle debate. They deaden social science by choking off one source of the genuine differences of opinion that are its lifeblood. Overt censorship of research is uncommon, probably because it is an obvious affront to academic norms. Less striking forms of censorship directly affect many more academics, however, and so may be more important. Easier to practice without detection and to disguise as "academic judgment," they serve to keep scholars from pursuing ideas that might undermine the egalitarian dogma.

A less obvious form of censorship, which has become somewhat common recently, is indirect censorship. It is accomplished when academic or scientific organizations approve some views but repudiate or burden others on ideological grounds. Sometimes the ideological grounds are explicit. Campus speech codes are a well-known example which, had they been upheld in the courts, would have made repudiation of the egalitarian fiction a punishable offense on some campuses. The earlier (unsuccessful) attempt to include possible "offense to minority communities" as grounds for refusing human subjects approval is another example.

Gordon reports yet others, including the National Institutes of Health's new extra layer of review for politically "sensitive"grant proposals and the University of Delaware's recent policy (reversed by a national arbitrator) of banning a particular funding source because, so the university claimed, it supports research on race which "conflicts with the university's mission to promote racial and cultural diversity."

Gordon also outlines in detail—as political scientist Jan Blits has done—the covert application of ideological standards to facilitate expression of some views but burden others. This form of indirect censorship, also falling under the rubric of "political correctness," occurs when university administrators, faculty, or officers of professional associations disguise as "professional judgment" an ideological bias in their enforcing of organizational rules, extending faculty privileges, protecting faculty rights, and weighing evidence in faculty promotions and grievances.

Recently, some American universities have invoked "professional judgment" as a pretext for reclassifying "controversial" scholarly publications in their annual merit reviews as "non-research," to misrepresent outside peer reviews in evaluating controversial professionals up for promotion, and to limit student access to these professors. Such thinly veiled bias publicly demonstrates the officials' own adherence to the prescribed institutional attitudes and their willingness to enforce them, not only protecting those officials from protest but also encouraging fellow members of the institution to toe the line.

Covert censorship is far more common than overt or indirect censorship. It consists of bias in the application of scientific norms when reviewers evaluate their peers' work for funding, publication, presentation, or dissemination. Individual ideological biases are found in all fields, of course, but the hope is that such biases remain small and will cancel each other out over the long run—hence the importance of a free and open exchange of data, theories, and results. What I have in mind is systematic bias and a pervasive double standard which impedes one line of research and accords another undeserved hegemony.

In one-party science, the disfavored line of work is subjected to intense scrutiny and nearly impossible standards, while the favored line of work is held to lax standards in which flaws are overlooked (called "oversight bias" in the psychological literature). Similarly, the disfavored idea is rejected unless it is "balanced" by including proponents of the favored view (even if that view is the equivalent of "flat-earth theory"), where the favored line of work is readily accepted for publication or presentation, even when it totally ignores the opposing literature. Getting a controversial paper accepted under such circumstances often becomes a test of endurance between the editor and reviewers (in coming up with criticisms) and the author (in rebutting them).

Submitting IQ research or grant proposals outside the narrowest professional confines exposes intelligence researchers to yet other biases, usually of the kind to which reviewers of the proposals will accept no rebuttal. The broader circle of critics in the social sciences often implicitly dismisses the legitimacy of research on intelligence itself by arguing that "intelligence" is undefinable or unmeasurable—as if the critics' own favored constructs (social class, culture, self-concept, anxiety, and so on) were as well validated and operationalized. Others now also seek to deny IQ researchers (but not themselves) use of the concept "race" because, they assert, race is not a biological condition, but is socially constructed.

The double standards can even ricochet back and forth, depending on the particular question being considered. Gordon recalls how sociologists failed to criticize sociologist James Coleman for omitting student ability from his analyses of school integration (which led to overstating the impact of integrated schools on black achievement—for sociologists a favorable outcome), but how they criticized him roundly for the very same omission in analyses of private versus public schools (which led to overstating the impact of private schools on black achievement— an unfavorable outcome). In short, in one-party science, scientific regard flows like political patronage to loyal and active party members, who can demonstrate their loyalty by being alert to hints of dissidence. Like all one-party political systems, one-party science becomes intellectually corrupt and arrogant as it gains confidence in its power.

The most insidious corruption to which one-party science leads is pervasive self-censorship, what involved researchers generally prefer to regard as "prudence" or "avoiding unnecessary trouble." Coleman has drawn particular attention to the problem of "self-suppression"—"the impulse not to ask the crucial question"—in research on race. In an example from his own research for the influential "Coleman Report," he describes his failure to conduct important analyses that might have produced embarrassing findings about the abilities of black teachers. Another way of avoiding unwanted results is to ignore certain data, subjects, or variables. Or unwanted results can be omitted, buried in footnotes, explained away, or simply ignored in one's conclusions. The most subtle form of self-censorship is deliberate avoidance of making crucial connections, or denying them.

Psychologist Richard Herrnstein has noted that it was his drawing out the implications of one such connection, namely, that some portion of (white) social class differences in intelligence is genetic, that sparked his public excoriation in the 1970s. Normally, scholars are eager to explicate illuminating connections between subspecialties. They are reluctant to do so, however, when these connections put in question the egalitarian dogma on race. Virtually all sociologists and economists ignore the literature on intelligence despite its central importance to core issues in their disciplines, such as inequalities in occupation and income.

Researchers in the various subfields of intelligence obviously cannot ignore the literature with impunity. Yet they, too, often prefer to stay strictly within the confines of their specialties rather than making crucial, but unpopular, connections, or they use language that obscures what otherwise would be quite obvious. Many psychometricians, especially those working for large testing organizations, avoid referring to "intelligence" and often seem reluctant to say much about the practical or theoretical meaning of the racial differences they observe on unbiased tests.

But even remaining within one's subfield is often not enough, for the field of intelligence itself is widely suspect. Hence some scholars explicitly disavow unpopular connections that critics might attribute to them. For example, they will argue in favor of the importance of intelligence for scholastic performance but then assure their readers, overoptimistically, that the racial gap "seems to be closing rapidly." The tenor of these preemptive disclaimers is clear.

While researchers in any field may lightly dismiss the credibility of key connections regarding race and intelligence, no one ever lightly endorses their credibility with impunity. Even those of us committed to candor are exceedingly cautious when expressing informed opinions on certain topics, especially the genetics of race.

Thus, publicly stated opinions of researchers about matters outside their subfields tend in one direction—to dispute or undercut the facts necessary for toppling the egalitarian fiction. What may be tolerable behavior at the individual level becomes intolerable bias at the aggregate level. Censorship—even self-censorship—requires justification, or at least apparent justification. On the whole, those who would squelch open inquiry of the egalitarian fiction base their justification on two assertions: (1) research on racial differences in intelligence has already been scientifically "discredited"; (2) inquiry into racial differences is immoral.

Point one asserts that the egalitarian premise is absolute truth and hence beyond scientific scrutiny. Point two is indifferent to its truth. Both counsel outrage at the very thought of the research. The claim that the research has been discredited rests largely on extensive misrepresentation that is often embarrassingly crude or casual—for example, contradicting arguments an author never made, while ignoring what was actually stated; attributing policy preferences to an author which are opposite of what the author actually expressed; or simply alleging fraud or gross incompetence without any substantiation whatsoever.

The claim that the research is immoral rests squarely on the view that, regardless of the truth, the study itself can only be harmful. In fact, some critics assert (mostly privately) that the greater the truth, the greater the danger it poses to lower-scoring groups, and thus the greater the need to suppress it. Despite their differences, both justifications for censorship often take the form of demonizing open inquiry by labelling it (and the people who practice it) as "dangerous," "fascist," "ideological," or "racist."

The study of race and intelligence is something, they tell us, that no decent person—let alone a serious scientist—would ever do and that every decent person and serious researcher would oppose.Thus, in a kind of Orwellian inversion, marked by what Gordon calls "high talk and low blows," the suppression of science presents itself as science itself. Intellectual dishonesty becomes the handmaiden of social conscience, and ideology is declared knowledge while knowledge is dismissed as mere ideology.

Neither social policy, nor science, nor society itself is served well by scientific silence on racial differences in intelligence. Enforcement of the egalitarian fiction has tragic consequences, especially for blacks. The outcomes are even worse than researchers of intelligence predicted two decades ago. The falsehood, because it tries to defy a reality that has conspicuous repercussions in daily life, is doing precisely what it was meant to avoid: producing pejorative racial stereotypes, fostering racial tensions, stripping members of lower-scoring groups of their dignity and incentives to achieve, and creating permanent social inequalities between the races.

Enforcement of the lie is gradually distorting and degrading all institutions and processes where intelligence is at least somewhat important (which is practically everywhere) but especially where it is most important (in public schools, higher education, the professions, and high-level executive work). The falsehood requires that there be racial preferences and that their use be disguised, wherever intelligence has at least moderate importance. Society is thus being shaped to meet the dictates of a collective fraud. The fiction is aiding and abetting bigots to a far greater degree than any truth ever could, because its specific side-effects—racial preferences, official mendacity, free-wielding accusations of racism, and falling standards—are creating deep cynicism and broad resentment against minorities, blacks in particular, among the citizenry.

Enforcement of the egalitarian fiction is not a moral or scientific imperative; it is merely political. It is terribly short-sighted, for it corrupts both science and society. However, just as the fiction is sustained by small untruths, so can it be broken down by many small acts of scientific integrity. This requires no particular heroism. All that is required is for scientists to act like scientists—to demand, clearly and consistently, respect for truth and for free inquiry in their own settings, and to resist the temptation to win easy approval by endorsing a comfortable lie.

Recommended Readings

Jan H. Blits and Linda S. Gottfredson. "Equality or Lasting Inequality?" *Society* 27, no. 3 (March/April 1990).

Robert A. Gordon. *The Battle to Establish a Sociology of Intelligence: A Case Study in the Sociology of Politicized Disciplines*. Baltimore, Md.: The Johns Hopkins University, Department of Sociology, 1993.

Linda S. Gottfredson. "Dilemmas in Developing Diversity Programs." In Susan Jackson, ed., *Diversity in the Workplace: Human Resources Initiatives*. New York: The Guilford Press, 1992.

Linda S. Gottfredson and James C. Sharf, eds. "Fairness in Employment Testing." *Journal of Vocational Behavior* 33 (December 1988).

Richard J. Herrnstein. "A True Tale from the Annals of Orthodoxy." Preface to *IQ in the Meritocracy*. Boston, Mass.: Little, Brown and Company, 1973.

Daniel Seligman. *A Question of Intelligence*. New York: Birch Lane Press, 1992.

Part III

Attribution and
Misattribution of Deception

9

Making Monsters

Richard Ofshe and Ethan Watters

Practitioners on the fringes of the mental health professions periodically develop new miracle cures. Most of these therapies lean toward drama, if not theatricality, and are often marketed through pop-psych books and talk shows. Clients are led to undertake exotic techniques, such as screaming their way to happiness or submerging in sensory deprivation tanks. When the techniques prove ineffective, the damage is usually nothing worse than wasted time and money. Interest in the "cure" soon fades. But sometimes, a different breed of innovation emerges from the periphery—one that frequently causes considerable and often irreparable harm. Lobotomy and "re-parenting" are examples. Criticism from professionals and the public has, in the past, been able to persuade nearly all practitioners to abandon the damaging treatments.

With hindsight observers wonder how the professions that spawned these either frivolous or dangerous excesses could have tolerated such recklessness. How could practitioners who used them have been so foolish or so arrogant and cruel?

Recently, a new miracle "cure" has been promoted by some mental health professionals—recovered memory therapy. This treatment leads clients to see their parents as monsters who sexually abused them as children. Parents have to witness their adult children turn into monsters trying to destroy their reputations and lives. In less than ten years' time this therapy, in its various forms, has devastated thousands of lives. It has become a nation-wide phenomenon—one that is becoming entrenched in our culture and the mental health professions with enormous speed.

The modus operandi of recovered memory therapy lies in uncovering supposed repressed memories from the client's past in order to cure their mental problems. According to practitioners, hundreds of thousands of adults, primarily women, suffer from the debilitating consequences of sexual abuse endured in childhood. Clients are told they have no knowledge of their abuse because their memories have been repressed. But full awareness of unrecognized abuse is the magic key to the client's return to mental health.

Practitioners of this type of therapy believe repression is a powerful psychological defense that causes one to lose all awareness of physically or sexually terrifying events. Not only is the event repressed but so are memories of the trauma's social context—that is, everything preceding and following it that would suggest to the victim that some trauma has occurred. According to the theory, virtually any mental disorder or symptom can result from repressed childhood abuse. Clients who respond to this therapy become convinced that they were ignorant of abuse which may have gone on for a decade or more. They may remain unaware of the trauma for perhaps thirty years, until they enter treatment where they discover their repressed memories. Once these memories are dredged up and accepted as real, practitioners encourage their clients to publicly accuse, confront, and perhaps sue those they believe to have been the perpetrators. These often turn out to be parents, siblings, grandparents, or sometimes groups of unidentified strangers. The inevitable result is the destruction of the families involved. Therapists feel obligated to do whatever is necessary to uncover their client's hidden traumatic history. The methods employed have generated profound controversies. Critics charge the therapy does not unearth real memories at all. Rather their origin is iatrogenic—therapist induced. Clients are essentially being tricked into believing that they are remembering events that never happened.

Two issues about this therapy should be considered. One is substantive, concerning the validity of the theories underlying recovered memory therapy. The other is an issue of policy. The substantive part of the controversy can be resolved by determining the answers to two questions: Does the repression mechanism exist and function as the therapy presumes? And are the techniques employed capable of producing false memories of abuse even if no abuse occurred?

The policy question lies in the mine field of political correctness. Sexual assault, particularly of children, has become starkly political in recent years. In the eyes of some, absolute belief in the accuracy and truthfulness of all charges is the only appropriate stance. In such a climate, one wonders if it matters if the therapy is valid or bogus? Because the therapy is becoming so rapidly institutionalized, it is questionable whether the conclusions from a reasoned analysis of it, or anything else is likely to affect its dissemination. Even if academics, researchers, and sophisticated clinicians were to conclude the therapy is harmful, would its use slow or stop?

Repression and Memory

The substantive controversy turns on the validity of the concept of repression, the central mechanism of the theory. Asked bluntly: Can the mind repress memories in the way these therapists claim? If repression is a valid concept, clients could be recovering long hidden memories of abuse. If invalid, repression is nothing more than a pseudo-scientific smoke screen for treatment techniques that create false memories. The concept of repression has been used in different ways in the mental health community for a hundred years. Freud employed the term to describe the mind's conscious and unconscious avoidance of unpleasant wishes, thoughts, or memories. Even under this conservative definition, the existence of repression has never been empirically demonstrated. Sixty years of experiments that would demonstrate the phenomenon have failed to produce any evidence of its existence. The notion of repression has never been more than an unsubstantiated speculation tied to other Freudian concepts and speculative mechanisms. The only support repression has ever had is anecdotal and contributed by psychoanalysts who presume the existence of the repression mechanism. Even leading psychoanalytic theoreticians recognize that the concept of repression is a meta-psychological principle rather than a testable hypothesis about human behavior.

In recovered memory therapy repression is the essential mechanism and the only acceptable explanation for a client's sudden report of abuse. Practitioners of the therapy have developed repression into a psychological phenomenon far more powerful than was ever suspected by Freud or anyone else until recently. Since 1980, the operational meaning of repression has been pumped up beyond all recognition.

In accordance with this robust repression concept, a person could, for example, banish awareness of the experience of having been brutally raped one or a hundred times during childhood. These distressing memories might be repressed serially, immediately following each event. Alternatively, all the memories might be collectively repressed at some time later, after the abuse had stopped. If the memory of rapes were serially repressed, a child could go from rape to rape ignorant of each previous assault. If memories were collectively repressed, the child could have retained awareness of the rapes throughout the years they were happening and repressed them as a group at some later moment. Whether serially or collectively repressed, the memories might not be "recovered" until years later under the influence of therapy. The only evidence supporting this concept is circumstantial and only comes out of the therapy sessions.

Modern memory research has demonstrated that normal recall of distant or even relatively recent events is subject to information loss and error for details. Recovered memory therapy's fundamental conception of how memory functions assumes that the human mind records and stores everything perceived. Under this assumption, it is reasonable to presume that minutely detailed recollections of the remote past are feasible. Freud's ideas about psychological processes influencing recall— what is remembered, distorted, forgotten, or repressed—all rely on this assumption. He also assumed that absent any adverse psychological influences, all information should be available to be accurately recalled— in present-day terms, it should be played back as if it had been recorded on a video camcorder.

Freud was mistaken. Scientific studies have revealed memory to be much more malleable than any recorder/playback analogy would suggest. Memory behaves in a reconstructionist fashion. Memories not only change over time but are influenced by the circumstances under which they are recalled. Memory is malleable for details, even for events that actually happened.

The properties of robust repression are dramatically different from those of accepted memory-related mental processes such as ordinary forgetting, intentional avoidance of a subject, and traumatic amnesia. While sharing certain superficial features with these phenomena, repression implies something distinct from each. By allowing repression to be confused with common memory phenomena, promoters of recovered memory therapy can more easily sell their theories to clients and the public. This confusion is important because it leads those being offered or told about recovered memory therapy to conclude that they comprehend what therapists mean by repression and mistake it for undisputed memory phenomena.

Everyone has experienced normal memory decay over time. Forgetting can include failing to remember an event or only recalling portions of it. Research demonstrates that the normal process of forgetting involves time-dependent memory decay. Repression, on the other hand, is an all or none phenomenon—now you see it, now you don't. Repression will cause the knowledge of the event to disappear entirely from awareness, perhaps only minutes after it happened. Someone who remembers only broad outlines of a distant, meaningful event is demonstrating normal memory. Simple failure of perfect recall or recall of only gross characteristics of distant events is not repression as the mechanism appears in recovered memory therapy.

It is also a common experience to remember an event after not having recalled it for years. The event may or may not be a distressing one. Consider a forty-five year old man who for the first time in twenty years thinks about the painful day of his father's funeral when he was eleven. For the first few years after the funeral the child may have periodically thought about that day, but with the passage of time he thought of it less often until eventually the gap lengthened to twenty years.

Not thinking about something for a long time is not the same as having repressed it. If the adult had repressed the memory in the manner suggested by promoters of recovered memory therapy, he would have become entirely ignorant of having attended the funeral and perhaps even of his father's death. If asked about the event, he would have said he was certain that there was none or absolutely sure that he did not attend. The person who simply had not thought about the funeral for twenty years would not have lost awareness of his father's death and, if probed, could have recalled the funeral. Due to normal memory decay, some details would likely be missing from his recollection.

A third common memory phenomenon is the motivated avoidance of a subject. In everybody's life there are moments or episodes one would prefer not to discuss or even think about because they were humiliating, guilt provoking, frightening or emotionally painful. The twenty year gap in conscious attention to one's father's funeral could very well have been caused by motivated avoidance. Avoiding a subject does not mean that its memory is buried in the unconscious and is inaccessible.

Amnesia induced through psychological trauma, that is, selective amnesia, is the memory phenomenon most easily mistaken for, or passed off as repression. Traumatic amnesia is the unusual but frequently reported phenomenon of becoming amnesiac for certain details or portions of a terrifying event. This mechanism describes, for instance, the inability of a teenage girl who endured a terrifying knife-point rape to recall many of its step-by-step events and her inability to give an accurate and complete narrative even shortly afterwards. The most straightforward explanation for memory disruptions of this type is that the person became so terrified by the experience that the normal biological process underlying information storage was disrupted. The cause of traumatic amnesia may resemble what happens during an alcohol induced "blackout." High levels of alcohol toxicity are known to cause a disruption in the bio-chemical process of memory. No information is stored in long-term memory during the period of the "black-out." A person experiencing an alcohol "blackout" will recall events up to the point at which long-term memory ceased to function. Later, the person knows that memory loss occurred.

Robust repression differs from traumatic amnesia in that repression supposedly leaves the person utterly unaware of the entire terrifying event and the circumstances that led up to and followed it. A woman unable to recall certain details of a life-threatening rape has not forgotten all that happened during the rape nor has she forgotten her terror. She remains painfully aware of the brutality of the assault, even if some of its elements can not be remembered.

Repressed memory therapists are not concerned with half remembered events of trauma induced amnesia and if a client clearly recalls instances of sexual exploitation, these practitioners remain uninterested. The only brutalization that truly matters to these therapists is abuse so devastating that it was repressed and is therefore entirely unknown and not even suspected when the client begins treatment. Any pre-therapy memories of childhood—painful, pleasant, or otherwise—are assumed to be nothing but facades hiding the truth. The accounts produced by recovered memory clients illustrate how the robust repression phenomenon differs from recognized memory processes and from the psychoanalytic concept of repression. Repression, in these accounts, turns out to be no less than psycho-magic.

A typical example is that of one thirty-eight year old woman who came to believe that she had accessed numerous repressed memories of being raped under a variety of circumstances. She was convinced that she remembered her knowledge of the rapes disappearing at the conclusion of each event. In one account, she felt her awareness of having been raped pass into her unconscious as she climbed the stairs from the basement where the rape supposedly occurred. Because of the magical mechanism of repression, when she entered the kitchen at the top of the stairs, she appeared composed and normal to her family. All her accounts were arranged so that awareness was blocked from her consciousness at the conclusion of the traumatic scene as if a curtain descended over it. This pattern of repeated, instantaneous repression supposedly explained why her childhood seemed so placid to her siblings, parents, friends and in her own pre-therapy accounts. The accuracy of many of this woman's memories were verifiable because she saw her siblings also being raped in numerous hypnotically recovered scenes. Her siblings, who were not in therapy, denied that the rapes ever happened. Her siblings' denials forced the woman to claim that they had repressed their memories and only she knew the truth. The denials did not shake her confidence in her therapy.

In some instances repression works in an entirely different fashion. Many clients of recovered memory therapists come to believe that they suffered strings of abusive acts lasting years and were aware of them throughout most of their childhood. In these scenarios the recalled abuse might start as early as shortly after birth and continue into their teens. Invariably, victims never confided the abuse to anyone. If groups were involved, no other victims ever told and perpetrators were never caught. At a certain age all knowledge disappeared from consciousness. Exactly why awareness of the abuse suddenly disappeared is unspecified or explained as somehow due to the activities of an evil group.

For these therapists the repression concept is all powerful. In the end, repression does whatever therapists need it to do. For practitioners, repression rationalizes the existence of any therapy-elicited allegation, whether a single sexual act done to an infant or a toddler, incest continuing for a decade, multiple gang rapes, or ritual cannibalism and murders. The robust repression concept is devoid of either scientific corroboration or independent corroboration of clients' accounts. Once defined through it's use in the therapy, robust repression appears to be science-fiction rather then science.

Influence of Procedures

To recover repressed memories, therapists employ procedures such as hypnosis, guided fantasy, automatic writing, strategic use of support groups, suggestion, interpersonal pressure and old fashioned propaganda, that is, directing clients to seemingly authoritative books in which the therapist's theory is advertised. Recovered memory therapy is an example of the maxim that those who ignore history are doomed to repeat it. Early in his career Freud used some of the same techniques today's recovered memory therapists employ—specifically, hypnosis, interpersonal pressure, leading, and suggestion. He too produced accounts of early childhood sexual abuse. Patients never spontaneously told such tales nor did they ever tell complete stories without strong pressuring. In Freud's words, he could obtain these stories only "under the most energetic pressure of the analytical procedure, and against an enormous resistance." Almost perversely, Freud's confidence in the accounts grew in direct proportion to the amount of pressure he had to apply before patients provided him with tales of sexual abuse during the first years of their lives.

At first Freud was greatly impressed by the tales he obtained and quickly claimed a breakthrough for his psychoanalytic method of therapy. Eventually, however, he recognized that his methods were invariably yielding false statements from all of his patients. While he always maintained his confidence that some of his patients had actually been sexually abused during childhood, he realized that even these patients were confabulating accounts of early childhood sexual scenes. His realization that all eighteen of his patients invariably confabulated accounts of early childhood sexual abuse raised a serious question about the validity and value of his psychoanalytic treatment method. He needed a theory to support his already published claim that the new method was an important innovation. Only this would save his faltering career. As Freud put it, "Perhaps I persevered only because I had no longer any choice and could not then begin at anything else."

He then had to consider the possibility that his analytic method was causing patients to report false accounts of sexual scenes—that he was pressuring or suggesting these scenes in some way. Freud rejected this possibility out-of-hand and eventually concluded that his patients' accounts of sexual abuse stemmed from sexual instincts expressing themselves from within the unconscious. He convinced himself that the cause of all forms of mental illness (and many physical illnesses) was reflected in the patient's fantasy life. His psychoanalytic method would cure it all. This self-serving conclusion salvaged something of great significance of his new treatment method and became the basis for much of modern of psychotherapy. Because Freud did not appreciate the danger of what is now known as "experimenter effects"—the influence of a researcher's expectations on a subject's behavior and the perception of that behavior—he could summarily reject the possibility that his treatment method was in essence causing the patients' fantasies.

In light of the moral and scientific paradigms prevalent in his time, Freud's conclusion that sexual deviance led to mental illness in some manner was not surprising. He shared his era's orienting moral perspective—essentially that sexual deviance was sure to be punished. Among the most seriously held ideas about mental illness in Freud's time were the notions that it was caused by either masturbation or coitus interruptus. In promoting his analytic method, Freud was merely seeking to distinguish himself from competitors for status and recognition. His writings about human psychology are shot through with assumptions about instinctual drives finding expression in human behavior and shaping it. Fighting against these drives will cause mental illness. It is quite likely that Freud communicated his strongly held assumptions and expectations about instinctual drives to his patients through questioning and interacting and that he unknowingly introduced and shaped the sexual contents of their fantasies. He was then correct to conclude that all of his patients were producing some fantasy material, but he failed to understand that his assumptions about human nature and the role of sex were causing the particular contents of their confabulated accounts of sexual abuse.

Freud's initial mistake of classifying pseudo-memories as factual accounts is chillingly similar to what is happening today in recovered memory therapy. Fortunately, examining the mechanisms of a contemporary phenomenon is much easier than conducting a retrospective analysis of Freud's techniques. Descriptions of the therapy's procedures are published in practitioners' books, articles, training tapes, and lectures on recovered memory therapy. In addition to the therapists' revelations, interviews with clients fill in important details of the picture of what transpires during treatment sessions and the pressures to which the clients are subjected. Therapists must first convince clients that they are in need of therapy. Early in the treatment they establish their special ability to identify the stigmata signaling repressed memories, which include classic symptoms of mental illness as well as a variety of commonplace physical symptoms, certain attitudes, and certain behaviors. In addition to obvious signs of major mental illness, "warning signs" of hidden abuse can include physical symptoms such as headaches, stomach pain, asthma, dizziness, and pelvic pain.

Lists of attitudes and behaviors that imply repressed memories are usually long and contain some quite exceptional statements, such as having a phobia about closing stall doors in bathrooms or awakening from sleep and attacking one's bed partner. Symptoms also include indications so general that they could apply to almost anyone—difficulty in maintaining a relationship, general feelings of dissatisfaction, liking sex too much, lack of career success, and fear of dentists. The presence of only a few symptoms is enough for someone to be considered a candidate for the therapy.

The first step in the cure is getting the trusting, unaware but possibly resistant, client to agree that brutalization probably did occur—most likely by a relative. Any shock or disbelief the client may express only confirms the reality of the abuse, the therapist tells them. The therapist's expectations predict the direction of the treatment. The client responds to techniques that encourage guesses, speculation, and confabulation. What starts as a guess about what type of abuse might have caused their present emotional problems, grows into guessing which relative committed the abuse. Repetitive retelling and reshaping of this account can transform a "perhaps" into a "for sure" and can thereby create a sense of certainty. The process may culminate in elaborate fantasies about schemes by parents, neighbors, teachers, or any other adults who were around during the client's childhood. It is now commonplace for clients to eventually arrive at the belief that they have repressed involvement in a satanic cult's rituals, involving murder of infants and cannibalism. Some therapists estimate that more than 15 percent of repressed memory therapy clients remember such brutal scenes. This estimate may well be very conservative.

Clients begin therapy with no awareness of the abuse that is supposedly at the root of their disorders. They are blank canvasses on which the therapists paint, using the techniques of the therapy. Studies have shown that people are most susceptible to suggestion when unsure about the matter at issue. New clients, being completely ignorant of what repressed memories their minds might contain, are exceedingly vulnerable to influence. Studies show that memories of details of actual events, even quite recent ones, are subject to gross distortion when pressure or subtle suggestion is used to change perceptions. Research also documents that entirely false memories can be created with minimal pressure or suggestion. For instance, subjects have "remembered" events from childhood that were made up by the researchers. Research into interrogations of crime suspects also shows that it is possible to lead psychiatrically normal suspects to "remember" committing a murder they did not commit. In both laboratory and field settings, once test subjects accept the premise that an event occurred, many confabulate appropriate details that make the memory seem real.

The process of recovered memory therapy is lengthy and offers the therapist innumerable opportunities to manipulate a client. The client/therapist relationship is ideal for influencing the attitudes and beliefs of the needy client. Even subtle pressure—signaling expectations or leading questions—can easily lead to conformity. It may take months to lead a client to the repressed memory root of the problem. A client may be told that recent dreams, or dreams remembered from childhood, are but tip-of-the-iceberg expressions of buried secrets.

A therapist may begin by focusing on a client's feeling, however vague, that someone made them uncomfortable in childhood or on an image of a silhouetted figure moving through their bedroom doorway. Any hostility the client may feel toward a parent may be explained as a sign that the parent did something to them far more terrible than the client presently knows. One or more of the pop-psychology books that report miraculous cures flowing from the "discovery" of such memories may be recommended by the therapist. In effect therapists prep these victims-in-training for key turning points in their therapy drama. Clients become sufficiently knowledgeable of the therapy's plot-line that they can improvise their way through the next scene. Often this prepping is done directly by the therapist or through books written by other practitioners of recovered memory therapy.

The training can also be done indirectly via victim-support groups in which long term clients pass on knowledge to newcomers. Knowledge of the expected twists and turns in the course of therapy can be acquired almost by osmosis just by being part of America's talk-show and tabloid culture in which stories of repressed memory discovery are told and retold.

The books recommended to victims-in-training prepare them to know among other things:

- How they should feel when a memory takes over;
- How to use vague and subtle sensations of uneasiness to license speculations about abuse;
- How mundane events can be triggers for memories, that is, serve as stimuli for engaging in fantasy;
- How "body memories"—literally, compelled physical re-experiencing of the pain of abuse—can be excepted to happen at certain points;
- How to use display of emotional suffering to legitimate reclassifying a guess, dream, or fantasy as a recovered memory.

Clients discover that playing the sexual abuse victim is a both demanding and engaging role. They do not realize that they have become involved in a living-theater psychodrama with their therapist, support groups, and family of orientation. In this exercise they eventually become committed to the role of victim and will emote. Whatever doubts they may have are subordinated to the therapist's judgment, the images they have fantasized, the stories they have confabulated, and the identity they have developed through participation in the course of this process.

In the repressed memory movement nothing is as pure and holy as a good cry or display of emotional pain. Clients who allow themselves to play the part of victim and describe an imagined rape scene set themselves up for strong feelings of distress. Allowing the release, that is, display, of the emotions appropriate to a rape increases confidence in the reality of the imagined event. Unaware of their ability to generate these emotions, clients use the display of emotion as proof of the truth of their fantasies.

Therapists also report that the memories their clients recover must be true because the emotions they display are so obviously real and powerful. These therapists are hardly unbiased observers. Even putting aside their commitment to repressed memory therapy, the proof of a therapist's skill and acumen rides on ability to elicit memories and provoke dramatic emotion. It is not surprising that therapists believe that these displays prove the existence of repressed abuse. In addition to showing appropriate emotion, clients can be expected to experience "body memories" at certain moments. Practitioners believe memories of abuse can be stored directly in muscle and skin tissue and that clients may re-experience the physical pain of the ancient abuse. Reports of body memories serve as added proof that the abuse happened.

As dramatic as these body memories may appear to be, research on the therapy's procedures shows why clients might experience pain for reasons other than budding repressed memories. The analgesic power of hypnosis, its ability to cause people to experience non-existent physical stimuli and to cause somatic changes, such as inhibiting perception of physical pain, has frequently been demonstrated. When hypnotized subjects are told they are about to be touched, perhaps even burned, with a hot object and then are actually touched with an ice cube, they will report feeling intense heat. Subjects can also be led to undergo somatic changes, such as raising skin wheals, altering body temperature, heart rate and causing warts to disappear at the direction of the hypnotist.

Hypnotic procedures arm the therapist with a powerful tool for influencing perceptions and beliefs, procedures that play an important part in recovered memory therapy. Hypnotic trance can be accomplished either through formal induction procedures, which are obvious, or via indirect methods, such as guiding visualization or relaxation. Hypnosis has even greater dramatic power to create false memories than social influence. But like social influence, hypnosis induces subjects to confabulate additional details to fill in the gaps in their memory. Hypnosis can accomplish exceptional degrees of cognitive influence. The scientific literature documents that hypnotized subjects routinely accept as memories scenes that have been suggested and visualized in a state of trance. These pseudo-memories help subjects develop confidence that these hypnotically generated fantasies are real.

In hypnotic settings, subjects prove sensitive to the social imperatives surrounding the hypnosis. Demand characteristics, as they are called, refer to the larger meaning and social structure that surrounds a hypnosis session. Clients engaged in past-life therapy, for example, bring into every therapeutic session their understanding of the assumptions underlying their treatment and knowledge of their position in a community of believers. Because of these demand characteristics, fantasies generated in past-life therapy predictably include costumes, props and backdrops appropriate for earlier times. Clients of recovered memory therapy too understand the demand characteristics of their particular therapy and are influenced by them. At the beginning of each session, clients already know the goal is to search out childhood scenes of a sexually abusive father, mother, sibling, or neighbor. Any guidance, leading, or suggestion during the therapy session is affected by the overriding demand characteristics of recovered memory therapy. When a hypnotized client pictures the silhouette of a person standing in a doorway, a therapist might suggest letting the figure enter the room. When the figure enters, the demand characteristics of recovered memory therapy will influence a hypnotized client to imagine a relative intent on sexual assault.

The memories that result from such therapy sessions, differ dramatically in quality and texture from normal recollections of long ago events and therefore must be regarded as highly suspect. The attributes of recovered memories match those of hypnotically induced pseudo-memories which can be so powerful and engaging that subjects sometimes volunteer that visualizing these scenes is "like watching a movie." With time and retelling, these visions tend to become highly detailed, in vivid color, and crystal clear. Details may include what people were wearing, what someone smelled like and specific dialogue. Therapists take such vividness and detail as proof of the accuracy of the memory when it actually implies the opposite.

Recovered memory therapy seems to have been produced by a series of mistakes. Most obviously, practitioners manage to ignore research showing that their principal techniques, social influence and hypnosis, cause false or grossly inaccurate memories. They refuse to acknowledge that three generations of researchers have tried and failed to confirm the existence of the repression phenomenon, in even its most conservative form. They ignore the fact that no evidence has been found to suggest that the human mind is capable of hiding from itself the kind of traumatic events elicited from clients in recovered memory therapy. Their assumptions about the way the human mind operates is known by specialists in memory to be nothing but pre-scientific folklore and myth. In short, these therapists are out of touch with modern research on the subjects on which the miracle cure depends. No one can doubt that recovered memory therapy is producing something quite significant— agreement with the therapist's expectations.

Therapy in Social Context

To a growing number of knowledgeable academic and clinical specialists in hypnosis, social influence, memory, clinical psychology, and psychiatry, it is obvious that the practitioners of repressed memory are misusing therapeutic techniques. Repressed memory therapy is a triumph of misapplied influence in which practitioners are demonstrating the power of their methods to create beliefs. Doubtless recovered memory clients are victims—victims not of their parents or their past, but of their therapists. While the outcome of the therapist's influence on the client is not always certain and many clients reject the suggestions, it has worked frequently enough to warrant recognition of its manipulative power and of the fact that recovered memory movement is evolving into one of the century's most intriguing quackeries masquerading as psychotherapy.

The distress some victims experience with the "discovery" of memories is only the first taste of pain to come. Because the memories implicate family and community members in horrible crimes, the trauma of this therapy radiates outward to involve often dozens of innocent people. The creation of two tiers of victims is one way in which this therapy differs from the usual quack cure. The primary victims are the therapists' clients and the clients' parents and others who appear in the memories are the secondary victims.

As a result of this therapy, adult children eventually will come to hold their parents responsible for imagined betrayal and to detest them for it. As part of the cure many are urged to insult, revile, defame, humiliate and sometimes ruin the reputations and lives of those they believe have tormented them. Some are advised to sue their parents and grandparents as part of the cure. Thousands of families have already been shattered. The possibilities for fracturing family groups are all being realized: the accused spouse is divorced; siblings are forced to choose sides; grandparents are denied access to their grandchildren; grandchildren lose contact with their grandparents and so on.

Practitioners of recovered memory therapy work the cure on both the unhappy and the seriously disturbed. Because the client learns to mimic the emotions of a brutally abused person, recovered memory therapy is exceptionally distressing. For those with serious disorders, the new cure is a needlessly painful and ineffective treatment. Recovered memory therapy diverts some seriously disturbed patients from effective treatments. In reality, most of these victims are probably caught up in a nightmare—an endless search for a not yet discovered cure for their actual disorder.

Those not suffering from major psychiatric disorders are likely to be relative newcomers to the psychotherapy industry. They do not realize that their therapists are primed to diagnose them in the current fashion and accept assurances that whatever their symptoms —anxiety, depression, anorexia, or malaise—their cause is repressed sexual abuse. Novices will believe that just because a practitioner is licensed he has the expertise to help, knows what he is doing and that the treatment is based on proven methods.

Most victims of the new cure remain in treatment for years. Some former clients have realized they have been tricked into accepting the beliefs required by the cure. Many of those who have had the courage to reject their supposed healers are outraged at having been processed by this cookie-cutter therapy. Some who accused parents on the basis of their recovered memories now appreciate the damage done to their lives and the lives of those around them.

Even if well-intentioned, the therapists are like the physicians who once bled patients in order to cure them. But unlike those physicians, who were limited by the primitive state of medical knowledge of their time, the promoters of repressed memory therapy ignore reliable research, misuse their authority and techniques, and damage the lives of their clients and their clients' families.

In this dispute about recovered memory therapy, there is no room for a middle ground. The mind either functions in the way the therapy demands or it does not. The techniques either uncover repressed memories or they create pseudo-memories. For PhDs and MDs on opposite sides of the controversy, the fight now starting may become the therapy world's gunfight at the OK Corral. Due to the extent to which the various forms of recovered memory therapy have infiltrated the mental health and social service professions, the seriousness of the allegations the therapies generate and the frequency with which damage occurs, if the therapy is invalid, the result of this shoot-out has far-reaching consequences for the future and respectability of clinical psychology and psychiatry.

Further Reaches of Memory Therapy

Believing any number of events from a client's childhood could have been repressed, therapists often press for more and more memories. Like modern-day Don Quixotes, they are convinced of the purity of their mission and the essential evil of what they are fighting. Unrelenting pressure from the therapist encourages invention of ever more bizarre memories. The recovered memory movement is constantly expanding its boundaries to accommodate the progressively bizarre and difficult to believe abuses imagined by the clients. At the outer edges of recovered memory therapy lie multiple personality disorders (MPD) and satanic cults.

Despite the promises of its promoters, the therapy does not result in lasting relief from symptoms of schizophrenia, depression, anxiety, anorexia, or other serious disorders, nor does it turn unhappiness into joy. Indeed, life's problems appear to get worse rather than better after the clients become convinced that they were brutalized in childhood. Cutting themselves off from their family and unbelieving friends, they may restrict themselves to a social world filled only with true believers. The stress of the painful process of recovered memory therapy may exacerbate pre-existing conditions or even precipitate disorders that had not previously been expressed.

Some long-term clients may be diagnosed as having multiple personality disorder (MPD). The frequency of this diagnosis has skyrocketed during the last decade. Often hospitalized, MPD sufferers find themselves subjected to a treatment regimen that is nothing less than spooky. They may be directed to host conversations among the various alter-personalities they have learned to role-play. Non-dominant alter-personalities may communicate with the therapist via finger signals rather than through speech. Therapists have clients build dioramas in sand boxes with plastic figures of dead bodies, coffins, witches, and black-robed figures. Clients may be expected to respond to therapist's commands to call up computer-like programs installed in them by a satanic cult— programs the therapist then tries to erase by using secret instructions learned from other MPD clients.

The behavior and symptoms of the estimated 25,000 MPD patients diagnosed since 1980 bear little resemblance to the symptoms and behavior of the few people similarly diagnosed over the last century. Some specialists in dissociative disorders believe that MPD is being massively over-diagnosed. Others believe that it does not even exist as a distinctive psychiatric disorder. One recent study of the earliest MPD cases, reported before repressed memory therapy became trendy, concluded that in all likelihood the whole history of the MPD diagnosis is a mistake, springing from the influence of hypnosis and suggestion by physicians. Experimental research on the relationship between hypnosis and

MPD has demonstrated that normal, non-symptomatic subjects can be induced to display the behaviors and symptoms of MPD in response to hypnotic suggestion.

Once a client is diagnosed as having multiple personality disorder, the therapist no longer has the problem of explaining why the client is not getting better. The accepted prognosis for MPD is that virtually no one recovers fully. The other strategy for managing the embarrassing matter of long-term clients' failure to recover relies on the quintessential anti-Christian evil: the satanic cult. Therapists who occupy the point positions in the movement started this trend by reporting discoveries of satanic cults responsible for their clients' brutalization. The cults were also supposed to have induced the clients to repress their memories of the cults' activities. The satanic cults that exist in the recovered memories of clients' childhoods are an especially beastly bunch.

Unlike youth culture groups that develop an interest in the occult and paint graffiti on walls or mutilate animals, the satanic cults likely to be recalled by clients in recovered memory therapy seem to exist for the sole purpose of brutalizing children. Clients routinely tell sordid tales of childhoods entirely controlled by satanists who forced them to perform ritual sex, and who are involved in baby breeding, sacrifice of infants, and cannibalism. Some clients report having been programmed to kill their therapists in order to prevent them from exposing the existence of the cult or to kill themselves rather than disclose information about the cult. Like the term repression, "programmed" is a bit of word magic. It lacks, however, even the suspicion of respectability attached to repression. Programming, a concept invented to mystify and cover over a great hole in pseudo-scientific theories of how evil groups exercise absolute control over people's lives, has been incorporated into recovered memory theory. The term refers to a mysterious process that supposedly produces ridged patterns of behavior and Manchurian-candidate obedience.

In the mythology of the recovered memory movement, programming gives satanic cults powers of control that border on the miraculous. The true miracle is how convenient the supposed existence of such cults turns out to be as an explanation for the inexplicable scenes produced by the clients' fantasies. Hundreds of police investigations throughout the country have failed to provide any corroboration of satanic cult memories. Kenneth Lanning, an FBI behavioral science specialist who has reviewed three hundred cases, makes the point, in his *Investigator's Guide to Allegations of "Ritual" Child Abuse,* that now it is up to mental health professionals, not law enforcement, to explain why victims are alleging things that do not seem to have happened.

The positions taken by the promoters of repressed memory therapy have gotten so bizarre, they nearly defy description. Take for example the recent report by Cory Hammond, PhD, one of the prominent figures in the movement. In a recent day-long training session for therapists, Hammond reported on cases of clients who were programmed as children by satanic cults and on the origins of the programming techniques that were used. From these clients, he learned that the programming techniques were invented by Nazi scientists who developed the procedures on death camp inmates. As it happened, the Nazi researchers were also satanists. These satanic scientists were captured by the CIA at the conclusion of the war and continued their "research" in the United States. The CIA code name for the programming project was Monarch.

According to Hammond, the key figure in the development and spread of satanic programming in the United States is a Hasidic Jew and death-camp turncoat. As a young man he supposedly saved himself from extermination by being useful to his Nazi captors. Part of his appeal to the satanists was his knowledge of the *Kaballah,* (a work of Jewish mysticism). Somehow, Jewish mysticism integrates well with the beliefs of satanists. After the war, this man was also brought to the United States by the CIA to continue programming research. After graduating medical school, this Dr. Green as he was called, began spreading his programming techniques throughout the satanic underground. Hammond warned that many other satanic programmers have also gone to medical school and are working as physicians in order to have easy access to children.

Hammond described clients' recovered memories of being programmed. They recalled being strapped to gurneys at age two or so and having electrodes inserted into their vaginas, vision disrupting goggles put over their eyes, and sound played into one ear. They were shocked and tortured in order to instill in them unreserved acceptance of the cult's commands. Hammond shared with his audience the particular instructions that would lead their clients to reveal the satanist-inserted programming and the verbal instructions for erasing these programs. Hammond went on to suggest that the *Illuminati* are the international network that controls all satanist activities. Satanists themselves, the

Illuminati seek to take over the world, he said, and one of their goals is to produce an army of "Manchurian candidates" for use in the takeover.

It would be a mistake to write off Hammond's claims as coming from a lone voice in the wilderness. Other nouveau eminent figures in the intertwined recovered memory/ritual abuse/MPD tradition are prone to similar statements. Hammond revealed his discoveries to a large group of therapists eager to learn how to treat their recovered memory and MPD clients. Despite obvious ultra-right wing, lunatic left, and anti-Semitic elements, Hammond's account of an international satanic conspiracy was greeted with a standing ovation. The audience's ready acceptance of Hammond's intelligence briefing from the twilight zone is not explained by his eloquence or compelling evidence. Recovered memory therapists have been telling audiences about the satanic underpinnings of clients' problems for years.

The therapists who are creating these and other bizarre fantasies have painted themselves into a corner from which they have no escape. If they admit that even some recovered memories are inaccurate, their position crumbles because they have no independent way of distinguishing between truth and fantasy in the statements their methods elicit. They would be admitting to what research on hypnosis and social influence demonstrates, namely that truth and fiction blend together into an amalgam that no one, least of all the subject, can ever again reliably separate. The percentage of truth in an hypnotically or massively influenced story can run from zero on up and so can the percentage of fiction. What is valid recall and what is pseudo-memory in the resulting story is unknowable without corroboration. Only pre-therapy accounts of a person's history can be treated as a normal memory with only the ordinary component of error.

Institutionalization and Longevity

It is unlikely that the therapy's practitioners will ever apologize for abusing their positions of trust, for failing to recognize the dangers of the techniques they are using and for neglecting to exercise appropriate care in the treatment of clients. This would be an admission that they have misled tens of thousands of people and convinced them that they have been horribly abused. It would be an admission that they have turned their clients against innocent parents and have caused enormous damage to the relations between their clients and their families. To do so would also be to admit that thousands of people have been hospitalized with the incorrect diagnosis of MPD—a condition that may not even exist. It would be an admission of massive malpractice for which they could be held accountable. Compared to other fringe psychology and psychiatric excesses the ghastly ménage-à-trois—recovered memory therapy, multiple personality disorder, and satanic cult conspiracy—represents an exceptional problem. The robust, super-powerful repression mechanism and the therapy's methods are on the verge of being institutionalized and thereby exceeding the relatively short life expectancy of other psychological quackeries.

One reason for the recovered memory therapy's spread is that it possesses an organizational quality that distinguishes it from the typical exotic cure. Normally, clients quickly learn that the fad does not fix their symptoms, lose faith in self-proclaimed psychological geniuses, and withdraw. This prevents institutionalization of fads and hastens their decline. Victims of recovered memory therapy, however, are more likely to tolerate therapeutic failure for a longer time because they have concluded that something particular and identifiable has happened to them. Therapeutic failure is explained away because of the unanticipated seriousness of what the client and therapist are discovering together. New revelations of abuse account for continuing therapeutic failure—this failure, in turn, provokes suspicions of even more serious abuses, which is confirmed by new memories which, in turn, accounts for continuing therapeutic failure, and so it goes.

A therapy's success in developing an institutional basis ultimately depends on the political trends that contributed to its rise. Broad concerns about child protection and feminist thought have contributed to the interest in these therapeutic innovations and their ready acceptance. Unfortunately, movements promoting social change face the danger, if not the inevitability, of stimulating opportunistic, zealous, and simpleminded spin-offs.

The constituencies created by the larger social concerns provide the muscle behind the institutionalization of repression theory and the therapy's procedures. The most startling example of this institutionalization is legislation and/or recent court decisions in fifteen states that now permit litigation based on recently recovered repressed memories. The unsubstantiated repression hypothesis is thus elevated to the status of fact. The new laws are tantamount to official certification that the phenomenon exists.

The potential impact is staggering since it opens the door to thousands of civil and criminal complaints. By alleging negligence on the part of a non-perpetrator parent, it is possible to involve homeowner's insurance policies and create deep pockets for people of modest means. At least 300 such lawsuits are known to have been initiated on the basis of recovered repressed memories. Widespread attorney interest is predictable.

Developments in psychiatry and psychology and changing market conditions have made these professions fragile. They are vulnerable to the possibility of fracturing into interest-group coalitions held together in uneasy alliances under their respective professional banners. Given these volatile conditions and the customary unwillingness of professionals to make enemies by publicly accusing colleagues of quackery, it is unlikely that many will strongly object to recovered memory therapy no matter how absurd they might privately think it to be.

The change in psychiatry is coming from the fact that virtually all significant progress in ameliorating symptoms of major mental disorders has been made in the past forty years through scientific research in bio-psychiatry. Genetic liability as a significant factor in vulnerability to major mental disorders is an established fact. This realization implies that valid treatment methods for major mental disorders will eventfully emerge from laboratories and not from the insights of charismatic, engaging, self-proclaimed psychological geniuses. Although progress has not been without its false starts and errors, and success is far from near at hand, the treatment of major mental disorders is being re-absorbed into traditional medicine and de-mystified as fast as dependable treatment methods are developed. This trend, if it continues, should have a substantial effect on both altering the prognosis for persons afflicted and diminishing the stigma associated with mental illness.

Progress in bio-psychiatry is causing a shift in the demand for psychiatric services away from talk-therapies and toward medical intervention in cases of major disorders. It is also forcing final realization of the uselessness of the dominant theoretical presumptions underpinning most modern psychotherapy—the role of the unconscious and the place of sexual instincts. Touted at first as a cure for all forms of mental illness, psychoanalysis, in the course of its history, has been in continuous retreat from the treatment major mental disorders. The symptoms of major mental disorders have never been alleviated by talk-therapy. Psychoanalysis has devolved into a thinly disguised process of re-socialization carried out under the label of medical or psychological treatment. The idea that the root of major mental disorders are found in interpersonal events in childhood is no longer supportable. The wish that discovering key events in childhood and releasing the supposedly pent-up emotions associated with them can be instrumental in curing major mental disorders also has become increasingly impossible to support in the face of the progress of bio-psychiatry.

These changes have left some physicians, psychoanalysts, and therapy practitioners scrambling for customers. Therapists who claim to be able to make people happy by curing their symptoms through application of the same logic, of finding the event and bleeding off the emotional residue, are also being hard pressed. Despite the fact that clients frequently agree that the therapy is helping, there is little reason to believe that anything more than attitude change is happening. The attitude changes clients experience need not have anything to do with the theory the therapist claims to be using nor with long-term relief of symptoms.

Competition for clients has intensified due to the proliferation of numerous types of counselors, alternatively certificated practitioners and self-proclaimed therapists. Short-run client satisfaction with their therapy may have a great deal to do with the confidence the therapist has in the method employed. The more confidence the therapist has in the therapy, the more successful the therapist will be in manipulating a client's attitudes. This success need not have anything to do with the validity of the therapist's theory or treatment method.

If all that matters is customer satisfaction, that is, attitude toward the therapy, self-proclaimed geniuses and their off-the-wall therapies should and do compete quite well with traditionally certified and trained psychotherapists. Most often it makes no real difference which theory a therapist uses.

Recovered memory therapies are thinly disguised, politically correct, pumped-up versions of the core Freudian speculation. Apart from beefing-up the concept of repression, their real innovation is in their far more powerful persuasive tactics. Since they are based on Freudian speculation it is relatively painless for universities to embrace them as the "new truth." Responding to the competition for clients and the demands of students for trendy treatment methodologies, clinical psychology programs in universities are moving away from tradition and are rapidly embracing recovered memory theory.

Legitimation of recovered memory theory by academia is contributing to the institutionalization of the therapy. Speculative robust repression theory is being taught in university psychology graduate programs, education school psychology programs, psychiatric residence programs, doctoral programs in clinical psychology, and at schools of social work, as if it were fact. Practitioners who have completed their education are being exposed to the theory and methodology in continuing education programs, such as the one addressed by Cory Hammond. Producing believing followers is likely to gain this fad a lasting position among practitioners if for no other reason than the sheer numbers committed to it. Using the persuasive techniques of the therapy, each new therapist is likely to produce new crops of clients who will recover lots of lost memories.

Even if a professional consensus developed and the informed general public became convinced that arguments like those developed in this paper are correct, it would probably not markedly retard the spread of recovered memory therapy. The professional and societal mechanisms available to protect the public from this sort of quackery border on the non-existent. The professions involved are too immature to have developed viable procedures for restraining excesses and have no way of prohibiting rank experimentation with humans.

In recent months the mass media has begun to report the other side of the repressed memory story, notably criticism by professionals and outrage by those who say they were falsely accused. If the media continues balanced coverage the most likely result is that therapists practicing the cure will become convinced that the world has misunderstood and rejected them. The elements of such a reaction are already evident.

In 1992 a grass roots organization, the False Memory Syndrome (FMS) Foundation, was formed in Philadelphia. It represents members of over 2,400 families who protest that they have been falsely accused. In the recovered memory movement the formation of FMS is classified as merely part of the backlash against women and children. Some leaders of the movement seem to regard anyone who questions their therapy as anti-female, anti-child, probably stupid, or worse. Worse is that critics are, to use Hammond's description, "dirty"—meaning they are part of the satanist conspiracy. Many professionals who have voiced criticism of the movement have at one time or another been accused of being satanists or agents of satanists.

These responses signal the collective paranoia of a social movement turning inward. The steps to isolation include rejection of the opinions of non-believers and increased reliance on only those who validate the ideology and claims of persecution. Once people become committed to an ideology, even one that masquerades as a testable scientific theory, the fact that it has failed is not necessarily perceived or it is often discounted.

Making therapists responsible for the quality of the services they render and the damage they cause is the only measure likely to inhibit the practice of recovered memory therapy. If therapists who elicit recovered memories and convince clients of their truth were obligated to demonstrate the validity of these accounts, they would be unable to do so.

As long as practitioners are not accountable for what they lead their clients to believe and what they encourage them to do, they will remain reckless. They have no need to notice the power of their techniques and will continue to believe the damage they are causing is of benefit to their clients and the suffering they cause parents is a just punishment. Their refusal to acknowledge what the scientific literature demonstrates about their methods and to face the possibility that they are dreadfully wrong may be thought of as a defense mechanism that has deep psychological, professional, and economic meaning—it functions to protect therapists from full awareness of what they are doing. In the parlance of recovered memory therapy, they are in denial.

Recommended Readings

Robert Hicks. *In Pursuit of Satan: The Police and the Occult.* Buffalo, N.Y.: Prometheus Press, 1991.

Elizabeth Loftus. *The Reality of Repressed Memories.* Address to the American Psychological Association, Washington, August 1992.

Harold Mersky. "The Manufacture of Personalities: The Production of Multiple Personality Disorders." *British Journal of Psychiatry* 160, no. 6 (1992).

Sherill Mulhern. "Satanism and Psychotherapy: A Rumor in Search of an Inquisition." In J. T. Richardson, J. M. Best, and D. G. Bromley, eds., *The Satanism Scare.* San Francisco: Aldine de Gruyter, 1991.

10

Incest, Freud, and Fraud

Edith Kurzweil

In his book *The Coming of Age of the Origin of Species*, published in 1880, Thomas Henry Huxley made the cogent statement: "It is the customary fate of new truths to begin as heresies and to end as superstitions." Psychoanalysis too began as a heresy. But a century after its formulation the question no longer is whether it is heresy or superstition, but rather why its decline has become such a fruitful source for academic research. For Freud bashing is in. By combining selective information from newly uncovered archives and previously available sources a number of philosophers, revisionist historians, and postmodern critics have postulated that the pseudoscientific qualities of psychoanalysis make it a fraudulent enterprise. But if these assorted skeptics are correct and psychoanalysis is as dishonest and as obsolete as they maintain, then one must ask why they keep wasting their time and bother scoring points by "proving" that Freud's theories are irrevocably passé, or, to put it crudely, why they keep on beating this dead horse.

Current Freud bashers benefit from the fact that psychoanalysts did not uncover the roots of the unconscious as Freud and his disciples had hoped; that documents and letters, whose existence was previously unknown and which reflect disagreements over theory and clinical practice are becoming increasinglyavailable; that the academic pursuit of textual interpretation has reached a fever pitch; that the early quarrels among the followers of so-called deviants and classical Freudians provide ample material for revisionism; and that these controversies themselves encourage the writing of biographies, which, in an age that

celebrates indiscretion, allow for the sort of speculation which the inductive qualities of psychoanalysis themselves incorporate.

For instance, the philosopher of science Adolph Grünbaum has spent
much of his life arguing with scores of Freudians whether or not psychoanalysis is a science, whether or not it is epistemically and clinically
viable, and whether or not epidemiological or physiological proof of
cure can be demonstrated. Phyllis Grosskurth, the biographer of Melanie
Klein, Freud's renegade spiritual daughter, has censured the Freudians,
in her book *The Secret Ring: Freud's Inner Circle and the Politics of
Psychoanalysis* , for continuing the practices of concealment Freud had
instituted to preserve his movement. Robin T. Lakoff and James C. Coyne,
in *Father Knows Best: The Use and Abuse of Power in Freud* , once
again demonstrate that Freud botched the analysis of "Dora," the first
case he described in detail. And John Kerr, in *A Most Dangerous Method:
Freud, Jung, and Sabina Spielrein*, enlarges on the story of Spielrein's
affair with Jung and Freud's intervention in it, which Aldo Carotenuto
had already brought to our attention in 1982.

The list goes on. For now, may it suffice to exemplify the debunking
of Freud by focussing on the central controversy stirred up by Jeffrey
Masson's claim that Freud abandoned his seduction theory. If Masson
were proven correct, then all of psychoanalysis, by implication, would
have been a hundred-year hoax.

Masson's exposé is based on disclosures from archival materials, on
speculation, and on conclusions from these. Of course, Freud's "science" as well is speculative. But whether or not psychoanalysts in the
confidential relation that is necessary for their practice are making un-
called for suggestions to their patients, whether or not they help detect
unconscious psychic mechanisms in them, and whether or not they are
totally ethical, has been the meat of the psychoanalysts' professional
exchanges and endless papers all along.

That Freud simultaneously invented a method, a theory of neuroses,
and a theory of the normal mind to ferret out the roots of the individual
and by extension social unconscious, and thus could not demonstrate
the validity of each of these enterprises by themselves, continues to confuse and to invite doubt. So does the fact that he locates his "proof" in
mythology and history, in literature and poetry, in religious practices
and everyday life. And a method that is as dubious as free association
makes it more difficult to prove or disprove fraud in psychoanalysis

than in the other social sciences. Still, this type of global speculation was part of the *Zeitgeist*, the time when such thinkers as Max Weber, Georg Simmel, Ferdinand Tönnies, and Emile Durkheim expected to be able to explain the repercussions of increasing fragmentation in modern society on individuals.

At present, the proponents and detractors of psychoanalysis both link current concerns to elements of Freud's biography; to components of his voluminous writings; and to specifics in the cultural and personal context. These interests themselves have spurred publication of previously closed correspondences, and have spawned new biographies as well as often violent disagreements among the biographers. Inevitably, the most controversial items are contained in the close to 10,000 known letters Freud wrote and which, in turn, continue to inspire speculations about his relations with his correspondents.

In view of the fact that the core of psychoanalysis resides in its practitioners' (and their patients') unconscious, it is not too difficult to impute fraud to Freud or to any one of his disciples. However, such fraud cannot consist of plagiarism or of "cooked" data. Nor could Freud have "stolen" the work of others. Still, he could have used his patients' memories selectively to ensure that psychoanalysis would be the ascendant psychology. He might well have done so, unconsciously, to further the movement. But fudging reality, or leaving any of his surfacing feelings and thoughts unexplored would have undermined his entire enterprise. And we can assume that one or another of his early disciples, who were a contentious lot and were constantly analyzing each other for the sake of psychoanalysis, at least would have pointed out Freud's lacunae in letters to one another if not to the master himself.

Yet, this is precisely what Masson has argued in his book *The Assault on Truth. Freud's Suppression of the Seduction Theory.* Essentially Masson is second-guessing the unconscious motives that propelled Freud in 1897 to change his mind about the location of his patients' psychic trauma—in fantasy rather than in actual seduction (or rape) by an adult (usually a father or other close, male). To prove his assumption, Masson focusses on Freud's shift in 1897 from the conclusions he had made in "The Aetiology of Hysteria," a paper he had read before the Vienna Society for Psychiatry and Neurology in 1896. At that point, Freud had argued that all eighteen of his patients who were suffering from hysterical symptoms had developed these symptoms in relation to some sort of sexual trauma during puberty; that these experiences awaken memories of earlier events; and that arousal of these memories will do away with the symptoms caused by premature sexual arousal, such as "stimulation of the genitals, coitus-like acts, and so on."

The reason for Freud's abandoning of this conclusion is, in fact, Masson's thesis. Thus he quotes the letter Freud sent to his confidant Wilhelm Fliess, who was considered by most to have been Freud's corresponding "stand-in" analyst, on September 21, 1897. (It is generally agreed that after this "turning point," Freud began the writing of *The Interpretation of Dreams* which was published in 1900, the year from which psychoanalysts date the birth of their discipline.) As was his custom in these letters, Freud elaborated on his moods and thoughts. In the following passage Freud makes the crucial point on which Masson bases his thesis:

> And now I want to confide in you immediately the great secret of something that in the past few months has gradually dawned on me. I no longer believe in my *neurotica* [theory of the neuroses]. This is probably not intelligible without an explanation; after all, you yourself found what I was able to tell you credible. So I will begin historically [and tell you] from where the reasons for disbelief came. The continual disappointment in my efforts to bring any analysis to a real conclusion; the running away of people who for a period of time had been most gripped [by analysis]; the absence of the complete successes on which I had counted; the possibility of explaining to myself the partial successes in other ways, in the usual fashion—this was the first group. Then the surprise that in all cases, the father, not excluding my own, had to be accused of being perverse—the realization of the unexpected frequency of hysteria, with precisely the same conditions prevailing in each, whereas surely such widespread perversions against children are not very probable. The [incidence] of perversion would have to be immeasurably more frequent than the [resulting] hysteria because the illness, after all, occurs only where there has been an accumulation of events and there is a contributory factor that weakens the defense. Then, third, the certain insight that there are no indications of reality in the unconscious, so that one cannot distinguish between truth and fiction that has been cathected with affect. (Accordingly, there would remain the solution that the sexual fantasy invariably seizes upon the theme of the parents.) Fourth, the consideration that in the most deep-reaching psychosis the unconscious memory does not break through, so that the secret of the childhood experiences is not disclosed even in the most confused delirium. If one thus sees that the unconscious never overcomes the resistance of the conscious, the expectation that in treatment the opposite is bound to happen to the point where the unconscious is completely tamed by the conscious also diminishes.

Masson (as do others) makes much of the fact that the 1954 edition of Freud's letters (edited by Marie Bonaparte, Anna Freud, and Ernst Kris) "included only 168 of the 284 letters available to the editors," and that the archives generally were closed. This is an ongoing point of contention between Freud experts who want total access to the archives and a few members of the so-called Freudian establishment who insist that they must maintain the confidentiality they promised the authors of the letters.

In 1980, Anna Freud and Kurt Eissler had chosen Masson to take charge of the archives. He did an excellent job of translating and editing what was published in 1985 as *The Complete Letters of Sigmund Freud to Wilhelm Fliess, 1887–1904*, although he had left the fold already in August 1981 after causing much publicity with his reinterpretation of Freud's abandonment of the seduction theory. (Fliess's letters to Freud have not been found.)

According to Masson, Freud had given up the actuality of child abuse and rooted it in fantasy rather than reality, among other things, to accommodate and cover up for his mentor Wilhelm Fliess, whose son Robert allegedly "believed that his father had sexually molested him at...the time Freud was writing to Fliess about seduction," but did not mention this matter until years later because it would have been in bad taste to do so about one's father. However, Freud's letter to Fliess does not support Masson's assumptions. It merely indicates that Freud changed his mind about his seduction theory. As for the speculations by Fliess's son, these remain speculations.

Unquestionably, at the time Masson wrote *The Assault on Truth*, he was in tune with the ideology of our *Zeitgeist*. Classical psychoanalysis had been denigrated in the culture as too expensive, emotionally and financially, as an elitist indulgence for the upper middle classes. Anyone who could show that it had been misconceived, that it was fraudulent, was bound to gain fame. Masson had been in an extraordinary position to do just that. He had been granted access to the inner sanctum, a privilege only a handful of insiders had enjoyed. It is not really possible to judge whether Masson consciously took advantage of his stroke of "luck"—motives cannot be judged by the hindsight of outsiders.

However, it is possible to conclude from Masson's subsequent public record that he enjoys the limelight. And in what has become our "politically correct" culture, he made all the right moves to attract acclaim. Most of all, he furnished much ammunition to that sector of the feminist movement whose politics of victimhood were then being institutionalized; and to those who were increasingly focussing on child abuse as the central source of other, ongoing abuses and social problems.

In sum, the publication of *The Assault on Truth* assured Masson the support of a large number of women, and of all those who were arguing for the special protection in courts of helpless victims, of minorities, and of the disadvantaged. And in his 1986 book, which followed on the heels of the first one, *A Dark Science. Women, Sexuality, and Psychiatry in the Nineteenth Century*, Masson extended his research to nineteenth-century medical practices in general. In her Preface to this book, Catharine MacKinnon notes the doctors' truly abusive habits and maintains that these "also were practiced during the Inquisition as liturgical justice, by the Third Reich as racial purity and medical experimentation, by the miltiary juntas of Latin American countries and Greece to maintain political power, and today by pornographers in the United States and worldwide as sexual entertainment."

In his own introduction, Masson states that these articles "represent the unspoken content of much of modern psychiatry" and that many modern psychotherapists (including psychologists, psychoanalysts, social workers, sex therapists, and so on) do not acknowledge but actually hold this attitude. These attacks on psychoanalysis are, of course, *ad hominem* and therefore cannot be proven to be either true or false. Masson's method is also a manifestation of the practice currently in vogue in American academic circles of employing American theorists' applications of Parisian discourse analysis, with its emphasis on texts rather than contexts, on the total picture. In our milieu these practices have led to the acceptance of ahistorical comparisons, and of a basic relativism at the expense of history.

In general, when this discourse is taken for granted by the media, a large segment of the audience—which no longer knows much about the past—is unable to differentiate fact from fiction. Masson's clever and informed use of Freudian texts combined with his lucid writing makes it all sound convincing. He argues forcefully, so that his selective use of materials, and his shifts (another application of French—especially Roland Barthes'—theories) are so smooth that only a close analysis can unveil the ideology that drives his enterprise.

Nothing Masson writes about is wrong or undocumented. He begins with the prehistory of psychoanalysis, and after focussing on the shift from "The Aetiology of Hysteria" to the renunciation of the seduction theory, he elaborates on the events surrounding Fliess's operation in 1895 on the nose of Freud's patient Emma Eckstein. He ends up connecting his interpretation of these events to Freud's criticisms of Sandor Ferenczi's 1932 essay "Confusion of Tongues Between Adults and the Child" which argues for recasting of clinical methods—for the analyst's empathic behavior with the patient (including selective touching and occasional kissing) rather than the abstinence Freud insisted on. Each of these issues, their theoretical and clinical importance, and their alleged roots in the personalities of Freud, Fliess, Eckstein, and Ferenczi already had elicited countless comments and polemics to fill the psychoanalyst's library.

Masson is not wrong when he states that Freudian analysts have come to adopt guild-like behavior, that they often blindly defend their discipline, especially to outsiders. However, his attempt to compel us to make an either or choice between rooting psychic trauma in the reality of actual childhood seduction and fantasies of such seduction is an oversimplification. Actually, Freud never maintained that children are not seduced in infancy, only that not all such recalling by patients in psychoanalysis is based on reality, that much or most of it rests on fantasy.

Of course, Freud and his disciples were groping in the dark trying to bring the unconscious productions of modern individuals to light; and of course they speculated, often absurdly, to make a science out of these elusive phenomena. Whenever they insisted that their inductions were scientific they (and their followers) skated on particularly thin ice. But Masson goes further than previous critics. He indicts Freud for his well-known admiration for the illustrious Jean Martin Charcot, under whom he studied in 1885/86, and his familiarity with the French milieu. He documents that among the 814 books Freud discarded in 1938, before fleeing the Nazis for England, were three major French works dealing with violence and sexual abuse of children to which Freud never referred, allegedly for not wanting to concede priority to these authors in 1896.

By emphasizing this point, Masson purports to "prove" not only that Freud was closely familiar with the issue of sexual abuse and that he had been under the spell of Charcot and his coworkers, but also that he was easily influenced by his mentors. This point then prepares the way for Masson's thesis of Freud's humoring of Fliess and of his acceptance of what are alleged to be blatant errors.

Contrary to Masson's assertion, Emma Eckstein's name has not been forgotten among psychoanalysts, at least no more than other psychohistorical figures and events. Wilhelm Fliess, however, would no longer be remembered were it not for his friendship with Freud. For his (crackpot?) notions of the transference of sexually repressed feelings to the nose obviously have not held up. Unquestionably, Freud was over-estimating his friend's abilities—both medical and intellectual. He certainly was too soft on Fliess after he found out that Fliess had left half a meter of gauze inside Emma Eckstein's nose, which led to profuse bleeding and endangered her life. And Masson accurately chides Freud for assuming, at the time of the operation, "that Emma Eckstein's hemorrhages were hysterical in nature, the result of sexual longing" and for his statement as late as June 4, 1896, that "there is no doubt that her hemorrhages were due to wishes." But is Masson convincing when he singles out "Emma Eckstein [as] the patient who provided Freud with the seduction theory"?

Throughout his book, Masson insists that some of James Strachey's emphases and odd phrases in his translation of the Standard Edition of Freud's works were due to hagiographic (and similar) motives; and that the suppression or withholding of publication of most of Freud's letters to Fliess by Anna Freud and Ernst Kris were due to their wish to uphold the genesis of seduction in fantasy rather than reality. No one doubts that Anna was protective of her father, although to what extent she was motivated by theoretical and professional convictions in order to "save" psychoanalysis is a moot question, which has been addressed by some "insiders" as well.

Masson invokes Ferenczi's challenge to the by-then prevalent methods of psychoanalysts' abstinence as the last nail on the coffin of psychoanalysis. Freud should have believed his patients, "for they were telling him the truth. The lies came from Freud and the whole psychoanalytic movement. Ferenczi, in 1932, was the one man who would have no part in this lie." Masson's conclusion is primarily based on the fact that Ernest Jones had been in analysis with Ferenczi, had come to dislike and then malign him (mostly in his biography of Freud), and that until Masson found a series of unpublished letters in Anna Freud's possession, this allegedly willful suppression was also upholding the suppression of the seduction theory. This is an admittedly crude summary of Masson's accusation of fraud by the Freudian establishment, but it gives the gist of it.

If Masson's accusations are correct then Freud indeed committed fraud, either consciously or unconsciously, in spite of his discoveries of the importance of the unconscious, of transference phenomena, regression, psychic defenses, and so on. If Masson is wrong, then he rather than Freud may be accused of fraud. Again, the problem seems to lie with Masson's formulation, with his either/or framing of the questions. In effect, Jones did malign Ferenczi, but this had been a well-known fact in psychoanalytic circles for many years. And Freud did call Ferenczi to task for his innovative techniques not long before Ferenczi's death in May 1933. But as André Haynal, a Hungarian-born psychoanalyst and historian of psychoanalysis living in Geneva, summarized:

> Freud's first meeting with Ferenczi [had] resulted in a mutual enthusiasm and a friendship that Freud (1933) was later to describe as "a community of life, thought and interests.... Many of Ferenczi's thoughts and conceptions reappear in the works of Freud, or, as Freud (1933) put it, a "number of papers that appeared later in the literature under his or my name took their first shape in our talks. Haynal went on to summarize this history and to show "that the two protagonists themselves never took up such clearly defined contradictory positions as are often attributed to them...that their relationship was made up of a tangle of complicated opinions and emotions."

Although the complete correspondence between Freud and Ferenczi is still not published in English, due not only to Anna Freud's objections but to the vissicitudes and costs of translations, and to lack of permission by Michael Balint (Ferenczi's analysand, colleague, and executor of his archives) and his heirs, Ferenczi's legacy was available in London. Masson must have been privy to all of it. Moreover, as Judith Dupont tells us in her introduction to *The Clinical Diary of Sandor Ferenczi*, which appeared in the mid-1980s, Balint had written an introduction to this diary in 1969 but wanted to have it come out at the same time as the correspondence.

In this diary, written between January 7, 1932 and October 2, 1932, Ferenczi focusses on the potential of a regressive technique to penetrate to the earliest infantile trauma. He argues that in the abstinent atmosphere Freud recommends, the analysand experiences a sort of re-enactment of this experience, a response similar to the one the adults had shown when they had denied their own participation in the child's original trauma. Therefore, the analyst's interpretations of earlier desires and longings unless accompanied by emotional involvement on the part of this analyst, was tantamount to its replay. Freud strongly criticized such involvement as too dangerous, but Ferenczi insisted that a corrective and manipulated emotional experience alone could lead to a reliving of the earliest sexual trauma and thus to its *Aufhebung*. Freud also disapproved of "mutual analysis," a technique which Ferenczi had agreed to with his patient R.N., who had apparently been sexually abused. Ferenczi abandoned this technique when he found that R.N. was a potentially destructive person who made insatiable psychological demands on him. In the process, however, Ferenczi developed what has come to be called his "active technique"—which included selective body contact.

Altogether, Freud's strength was in the development of psychoanalytic theory, while Ferenci's strength was in technique. Freud focussed on the psychoanalyst's abstinence, Ferenczi on the patient's controlled gratification. And Ferenczi elevated the emotional over the scientific elements in the clinical encounter. Differences as fundamental as these were bound to lead to a clash. Masson chooses to stress these differences; and he ignores Freud's agreement that some patients' sexual trauma is based in reality—although Ferenczi thought such incidents were more frequent than Freud did. Clearly, both extrapolated from their work with patients, some of whom at least were cured of, or learning to live with, their neuroses. The present polemics, however, are about the correspondence in which they discuss their work, about their attempts to improve it.

By placing the emphasis solely on the disagreements between Freud and his followers, Masson and his breed of critics disregard the fact that psychoanalysis did help some people and that most of the therapies they now elevate over and above psychoanalysis incorporate at least some of Freud's inventions. Moreover, psychoanalysis itself has changed our culture which, in turn, has altered the symptoms individuals bring into (psychoanalytic) therapy. So even if, as Peter Swales surmises, Freud had an affair with his wife's sister, how would that alter his impact on modern society?

Even if each of the Freud bashers' arguments were not slippery and could be proven, none of them actually step out of their argument long enough to examine their own motives and interests. Nor do they seem to be cognizant of the drastic changes in mores that have taken place since Freud's time. But their appeal is pervasive among many American therapists who, because they lack medical training, have not been admitted to the inner sanctum; among social workers, psychologists, practitioners of EST, of transactional analysis and the 250 other ways of committing therapy—including all those that insist on analyzing conscious phenomena alone.

Altogether, American populist tradition, which has come to include the belief in quick, therapeutic fixes, and eschews hierarchies, holds little brief for the "elitist" practice Freud and his disciples invented. And shorter sessions, innovative uses of the transference and countertransference may well be the way of the future. This certainly is as much a reason for the revival of Ferenczi's techniques as the publication of his letters, his diary, and all the other archival materials.

Whether or not Freud committed fraud in elevating fantasies of seduction over realities, whether or not he mistreated Jung, Adler, or any others of his contemporaries, or what motivated him to botch Dora's or the "Wolfman's" analysis, is not going to make a whit of difference to individuals who have been, or choose to be, analyzed. However, whatever may be the unconscious motives of the Freud bashers, their promotion of the downfall of psychoanalysis, in the present climate at least, will help promote their left-liberal image in the culture at large, and their acclaim among revisionists in the academy. Disagreements on certain questions between Freud and his disciples do not substantiate the charges against Freud, nor do they support the total rejection of Freud and of psychoanalysis.

Recommended Readings

Phyllis Grosskurth. *The Secret Ring: Freud's Inner Circle and the Politics of Psychoanalysis.* Reading, MA: Addison-Wesley, 1991.

Adolph Grünbaum. *The Foundations of Psychoanalysis.* Berkeley: University of California Press, 1988.

Robin T. Lakoff and James C. Coyne. *Father Knows Best: The Use and Abuse of Power in Freud.* New York: Columbia Teachers College Press, 1991.

John Kerr. *A Most Dangerous Method: Freud, Jung, and Sabina Spielrein.* New York: Alfred A. Knopf, 1993.

Jeffrey M. Masson. *The Assault on Truth. Freud's Suppression of the Seduction Theory.* New York: Farrar, Straus and Giroux, 1984.

11

Cyril Burt: Fallible Judgments about Deception

Robert B. Joynson

The British pioneer of educational psychology Cyril Burt (1883–1971) was first publicly accused of scientific fraud in 1976, five years after his death. Oliver Gillie, then medical correspondent to the *London Sunday Times* (October 24, 1976), reported that "leading scientists are convinced that Burt published false data and invented crucial facts to support his controversial theory that intelligence is largely inherited." The debate that ensued died down only with the publication in 1979 of Leslie Hearnshaw's biography of Burt. Hearnshaw, who had access to Burt's diaries, claimed that these provided decisive evidence of Burt's guilt, and concluded that the chief allegations were true "beyond reasonable doubt." His verdict was endorsed, without further inquiry, by the British Psychological Society in 1980.

In the last few years, there has been a remarkable revival of interest in the case of Cyril Burt, for very serious doubt has been thrown on the validity of the allegations. The evidence was examined independently by Banks in 1983, by Ronald Fletcher in 1987 and the present writer in 1989). These investigators all concluded that the charges cannot be sustained. The question of Burt's guilt has been thrown wide open and the Council of the British Psychological Society has announced in a Council Statement in 1992 that the Society "no longer has a corporate view on the truth of allegations concerning Burt."

No one can foresee how the debate will continue, but it seems unlikely that it will prove possible to restore the position which existed in

1980. Hearnshaw's confident verdict broke down basically because the evidence is, and must remain, incomplete. The case against Burt could only be substantiated if Burt, and his chief assistant, Conway, were available for questioning; and if Burt's raw data sheets were available for inspection. But Burt and Conway are both dead, and Burt's data have been destroyed. Under these circumstances, accusations of fabrication of data remain questionable.

The way in which Burt was condemned has also been found wanting. There is a basic injustice in condemning a man who cannot defend himself; and the Council of the British Psychological Society has, if a little late in the day, come to the conclusion that "it should not normally attempt to pass corporate judgment on the alleged misconduct of any member now deceased." Thus, even if a strong case against Burt could again be assembled, it is most unlikely that it would again be officially endorsed.

The posthumous condemnation of Burt destroyed his reputation, and undermined his life's work; and it is a matter for grave concern that the evidence should prove to be unreliable, and the procedure unjust. But the grounds for concern go far beyond the issue of justice for an individual, important as that is. The case has aroused wide interest, and much controversy, primarily because of its political dimension. Burt had exercised considerable influence on educational policy, and when he was accused of fabricating his data it was widely asserted that he had done so in order to support right-wing views on selective schooling. If this were true, Burt would have been guilty of a monstrous betrayal of science.

Moreover, the accusation attracted maximum publicity, and Burt's reputation maximum odium, because it was made at a time when controversy concerning the inheritance of intelligence was at its height. The questions of affirmative action and of black-white intelligence in America, and of comprehensive of selective schooling in Great Britain, were among the topics most closely affected. Thus a political interpretation was at once attached to the case, which varied according to the standpoint of the writer. *The Times* referred darkly to "the ideological foundations of the hereditarian position (November 9, 1976).

Hans Eysenck wrote in a letter to Marion Burt in 1976, "I think the whole affair is just a determined effort on the part of some very left-wing environmentalists to play a political game with scientific facts." Heim commented that "the pre-occupation of the left-wing with extreme environmentalism and of the right-wing with heritability...largely accounts for the axe-grinding dogmatism of the protagonist." (*The Times*, November 1, 1976) The relation between these political pressures and the accusations made against Burt is a central and unavoidable issue.

In 1992, Arthur Jensen provided a comprehensive review of the evidence to date. The aim of the present article is not to offer a further review, but to ask what the affair has to teach us about the social sciences in general, and psychology in particular.

Psychology of Scientific Investigation

How did it happen that first Burt's original accusers, then his biographer, and finally the Council of the British Psychological Society itself, all made such apparently fallible judgments in a matter of such exceptional importance, a matter in which psychology's reputation for scientific detachment was at stake? First, we must ask how mistakes and errors arise in the interpretation of scientific data in general. Indeed, all allegations of fraud and deception in science need to be considered in this context, for we can be sure that culpable deception has occurred only after the possibility of human error, whether in the accuser or the accused, has been eliminated. William James had some wise words on the subject of scientific discovery. In his essay "The Will to Believe," James stated that the investigator must care deeply about the outcome of his inquiry: "[S]cience would be far less advanced than she is if the passionate desires of individuals to get their own faiths confirmed had been kept out of the game." By contrast, indifference to the outcome of an inquiry was fatal: "[I]f you want an absolute duffer in an investigation, you must...take the man who has no interest whatever in its results: he is the warranted incapable, the positive fool."

But the "passionate desire" to confirm our own faith makes us prone to ignore evidence to the contrary, unless we are constantly on our guard. James concluded: "The most useful investigator, because the most sensitive observer, is always he whose eager interest in one side of the question is balanced by an equally keen nervousness lest he become deceived. Science has organized this nervousness into a regular technique."

Social scientists thus should not to be for their political or social values, whether of the right or the left, nor for their desire to see those values confirmed. Criticism should be reserved for those whose eager interest in one side of the question is not balanced by an equally keen nervousness lest he become deceived. Those who claim the authority of science must be prepared to demonstrate that they regard its "regular technique" as paramount; and that they are not ignoring or abusing that technique in order to further their own faith. But at this point an acute difficulty arises. The "regular technique" of science does not provide a rigid routine which, if slavishly followed, guarantees a valid outcome. There is always some latitude for fallible individual judgment, both in the application of the method and in the interpretation of its findings. Consequently, there may be disagreement about what the regular technique requires; and when passionate desires are involved, the disagreement can rapidly turn into furious recrimination.

In the aftermath of Burt's condemnation, the British Psychological Society organized a symposium to discuss "Burt's deceptions...in the wider context of scientific method in psychology." Blackman in 1980 drew attention to the role of personal judgments about experimental data, especially in relation to the assessment of the reliability, the validity, and the scientific significance of data. He concluded that "there are no fixed rules which provide even experimentalists with security and safety from making false or inappropriate inductive inferences about their data."

Selection begins in perception, in attending to some things and ignoring others. The process continues in experiment, with its carefully restricted and controlled situation. It is carried still further in describing the experimental results, for it is impossible to include everything which happens; and even if it were possible, it would be intolerably tedious. We have to select what we consider most relevant and ignore the rest; and what we choose to include, and what we choose to omit, can only be, to a large and uncertain extent, a matter of personal judgment. This long and unavoidable process of selection provides "the passionate desires of individuals to get their own faiths confirmed" with a magnificent opportunity to seize on every scrap of favorable evidence, and brush everything else aside.

The judgment of size and distance, like many perceptual topics, raises questions about the subject's "attitude." Roughly speaking, a subject may either attend to the sheer sensory input, such as the apparent size, shape, or color of an object (often called an "analytic" judgment); or he may report his perceptual impression of the true properties of the object, as he might judge in everyday life (sometimes called a "naive" judgment.)

Gestalt psychologists, who made so many important contributions in this field, have always maintained that analytic judgments are artificial constructions, only introduced to prove a theory, and never occurring without special instructions and training; and accordingly their theories were based entirely on "naive" judgments. In my own experiments I found that analytic judgments frequently appeared quite spontaneously, with no special instructions or training at all. What we like to call the given, the experimental datum, the observed fact, may be, not the whole truth, but just that part of which we like the look—an apt phrase in this context.

Even when we agreed what data are significant, there may be genuine disagreements over how they are to be interpreted. In the following instance, the data were obtained in an experiment originally undertaken with a view to confirming Helson's views on "central tendency" effects. In the case of size and distance, this would involve showing that, if the subject is presented with a series of target objects of varying size, targets around the average value of the series would tend to be judged accurately, whereas targets deviating from the average value would be judged with increasing inaccuracy; these tendencies varying with distance in predictable ways.

The questions at issue are difficult to settle because the "regular technique" of science does not provide an infallible set of rules which can be automatically applied. Individual judgment is required. It is also not difficult to understand how suspicions of dishonesty might arise, however unjustified. But the accusation of dishonesty should always be the last resort. First, we should explore the innumerable ways in which honest differences of opinion may arise.

Most of us resist the temptations to invent data because we do not merely want to confirm our own faiths, we also want to convince ourselves, as well as others, that we are good scientists. The omission of data, by contrast, offers an almost unlimited field for self-justificatory ingenuity. Omission, as we have seen, is part and parcel of the normal process of experiment, and a thousand innocent reasons spring to mind for omitting what does not seem to fit in. Did the subject understand the instructions? Was he distracted? Was there some failure in the apparatus? Were the responses correctly recorded? The possibilities are endless.

Even the decision when to conclude an experiment may be affected. There may often be excellent reasons for eliminating errant subjects. But it is the experimenter who makes the decision, and it is fatally easy to confuse good reasons with welcome excuses. In the matter of the omission of data, then, there is a large area where moral and technical issues are mixed up together, and where even the wisdom of Solomon might be strained.

Confrontation of Facts and Values

The condemnation of Cyril Burt took place when the debate concerning the inheritance of intelligence was at its height, and it will be instructive to recall some observations on the controversy which were made by a natural scientist who was not himself involved in it. In 1977 (that is, after the initial accusations had been made against Burt, but before they had been endorsed by Leslie Hearnshaw and the British Psychological Society), the presidential address to the British Association for the Advancement of Science was delivered by Sir Andrew Huxley, a Royal Society Research Professor in the department of physiology at University College London and grandson of the eminent Victorian scientist Thomas Huxley. The lecture was concerned with the importance of basing conclusions upon scientifically established facts, whatever our political or social values may be.

Huxley began by distinguishing "clues" from "evidence." A clue, he said, is an isolated fact, recognized as possibly significant to the problem in hand, but capable of various interpretations. Clues are indispensable in the early stages of research, when the scientist is considering what observations to make, and what hypotheses to frame. But clues remain capable of many interpretations, and further facts are needed to decide among them; they are suggestive not decisive.

Evidence, by contrast, is an organized arrangement of well-attested facts, if possible experimentally established, which leads to a compelling interpretation. It is easy to be led astray, especially in the early stages of research, by assumptions which lead to false expectations. It is important that the scientist not confuse clues with evidence, or reach premature conclusions through treating clues as if they were evidence. Thus Darwin collected many clues to evolution during his voyage on the *Beagle* in 1839, but spent twenty years testing and correcting his ideas before he was ready to publish in 1859. This was surely a classic instance of "eager interest" in the establishment of a preferred hypothesis being balanced by "keen nervousness."

Motive, if we are not careful, may disrupt the patient process of converting clues into evidence. Darwin's habit of recording observations unfavorable to evolution, lest he forget them, is well known. In his case, motive also featured spectacularly in the emotional opposition which his ideas aroused, both from conservative scientists who clung to the long-accepted principle of the fixity of species, and from theologians and others who saw a threat to the authority of the Bible and to morality. The question at issue in the famous confrontation of 1860 between the Bishop of Oxford and Thomas Huxley was whether a scientific question should be decided by factual evidence, or by what we might wish to believe for other reasons.

Andrew Huxley then said that he had sometimes asked himself whether any contemporary question could lead to a similarly dramatic and emotional confrontation between facts and values; and suggested that an instance was indeed to be found in the contemporary debate concerning the inheritance of intelligence. Any assertion of large natural differences in ability between individuals, or classes, or ethnic groups, was seen by some people, he said, as a threat to political ideals of equality, and was denounced as elitist or racist. Huxley delivered a scathing denunciation of "scientists who regard the assumption of equal inherited ability as something which does not require experimental evidence to establish—and which it is politically wicked to question, because the conclusion might disagree with their social and political preconceptions."

Huxley went on to say that the scientist has "a special claim to be listened to as long as what he says is soundly based on actual evidence, but he forfeits that claim if he presents preliminary or uncertain results—that is to say, clues—as if they were well supported by evidence, or, more important, if he selects or slants his results so as to support a view which he holds on other grounds, however meritorious or otherwise that view may be."

In his response to Huxley's lecture, Young alleged, in an article in 1977 in the *Times Higher Education Supplement,* that so far as Burt was concerned "the values, theory and policy came first" and the findings were created, embroidered or tidied up to suit them. Huxley replied that, if this were true, it would be an instance of that which he condemned. But, he added, "I do not myself believe it is true."

Huxley's parallel with the events of 1860 likened the hereditarians to the Darwinians, as the party of those who appeal to factual evidence;

and the environmentalists to the theologians, as the party of those who prefer "what we might wish to believe for other reasons." But historical parallels rarely hold exactly, and the position today is by no means so black-and-white as when Thomas Huxley did battle with the Bishop of Oxford (if indeed it was quite so black-and-white then). We are all to an extent torn between facts and values.

Huxley himself pointed to a significant divergence when he said that the evidence to support the case for or against the inheritance of ability was not to be compared with the overwhelming body of evidence which Darwin had amassed in 1860: "Even the strongest proponent of substantial inherited differences is aware that a large social component also exists."

A further important distinction to be made is that the case for heredity in the 1970s was not, as was the case for natural selection in the 1860s, a new challenge to an old orthodoxy. It goes back to Galton's hereditary genius of 1869; and among the pioneers of psychometrics there was from the beginning a widespread belief that mental tests came close to measuring a "natural" level of intelligence, independent of schooling. There was also a readiness to accept favorable "clues" which today we should find unconvincing, as when Spearman wrote to Burt about the latter's first paper in 1909 that "the evidence as to heredity of intelligence is very striking."

In spite of the uncertainties, mental tests were soon used to select out those believed to be naturally gifted or naturally backward; and by the 1920s and 1930s this had become a widely accepted practice, especially in Great Britain where psychologists were often consulted on issues of national education. A belief in the importance of heredity was thus part-and-parcel of the whole psychometric movement; and by mid-century was well established despite the limitations of the evidence.

Psychometrics, however, had always had its critics, and they remained vocal today. At Cambridge, England, objections focussed on the statistical analysis of tests and their reliability, while Otto Zangwill expressed concern in 1950 about premature application. In America, too, there was interest in the role of the environment, especially in early development. During the 1960s and 1970s, it was increasingly asserted that the psychometric movement in general, and the belief in the importance of inheritance in particular, were inspired, not by cogent scientific evidence, but by right-wing political convictions.

Leon Kamin's book *Science and Politics of IQ* was a notable expression of this critique. Kamin reviewed the whole body of hereditarian evidence in great detail, and concluded: "There are no data sufficient for us to reject the hypothesis that differences in the way in which people answer the questions asked by testers are determined by their palpably different life experiences." He also argued that the whole mental testing movement had been fostered by men with strong right-wing values who had misused it for political purposes as in the control of immigration to the United States. Pseudo-science was being used to justify and implement political policies.

Kamin's conclusions were seen by many as a travesty of the empirical evidence in the field. But an experimental psychologist at Cambridge, considered that Kamin had performed "a notable service by subjecting the evidence on the heritability of intelligence to searching and critical analysis," and added that "both in quality and quantity the evidence for the heritability of IQ is very much less than had generally been suggested. The data are sparse rather than plentiful, and at best persuasive rather than decisive." It seems, then, that a not implausible case might be made for inverting Huxley's parallel. Might not hereditarians be seen as a premature orthodoxy, swayed by wishful thinking, and environmentalists as the new scientific challenge?

There is much to support Kamin's argument. His fundamental criticism—that the hereditarian standpoint may sometimes be adapted in part for political rather than empirical reasons—is both true and important. Rose warned in an article in the *Times Literary Supplement* in 1992, against assuming that "hereditarian educational psychologists are scientists following where the data inexorably lead, unmoved by their social and political implications." In this respect, then, Huxley's parallel needs qualification. But we must equally beware of assuming that environmentalists are scientists "following where the data inexorably lead, unmoved." There is an obvious possibility in Kamin's case that the bias derives from loyalty to the left. Indeed, Rose, Kamin, and Lewontin, in *Not in Our Genes*, preface their critique by announcing their politics: "We share a commitment to the prospect of the creation of a more socially just—a socialist—society." The beam in their own eye bears a remarkable resemblance to that which they detect in the eye of their opponents.

The truth is surely that none can claim a monopoly of scientific virtue. All are exposed to a struggle between political preference and loyalty to science. There is a very real possibility that supposedly scientific findings may be a cloak for political values, whether of the right or left. This raises acute problems for a scientific psychology. We have to recognize that the "regular techniques" of science cannot yet provide, in this field, an objective assessment of the evidence wholly independent of human judgment; and where human judgment is involved, social and political values may enter.

If we follow William James, we shall not condemn an "eager interest in one side of the question." We shall recognize that this may be the spur to discovery. J. M. Thoday, head of the department of genetics at Cambridge, contended in an article, "Probity of Science: The Case of Cyril Burt," in *Nature* in 1981: "[I]deological motivation may have a place in science. If strong distaste for scientific conclusions leads to honest and intelligent criticism of the data base or logical base for those conclusions, this is to the good." Yes, indeed; but who is going to tell us when the criticism is honest and intelligent, and when not? The "elitists" or the "egalitarians"? The "eager interest" of the parties is unfortunately not always balanced by an equally "keen nervousness."

Kamin and those who think like him are, of course, politically correct, but their language has sometimes been distinctly unparliamentary. Kamin was not content to point to prejudice; he charged dishonesty. His book *The Science and Politics of IQ* begins with a sweeping insinuation against hereditarians in general: "Patriotism, we have been told, is the last refuge of scoundrels. Psychologists and biologists might consider the possibility that heritability is the first."

In the 1970s to be accused of dishonesty had become an occupational hazard for hereditarians, and there was an audience ready and willing to believe such accusations, however flimsy the evidence. So there is an obvious alternative to supposing that Cyril Burt fabricated his data, namely, that he was a victim of left-wing hostility. There is strong evidence for such bias in at least some of Burt's accusers, notably Barbara Tizard.

In a memoir of her husband, *Child Development and Social Policy: The Life and Work of Jack Tizard*, she describes him as a "passionate egalitarian...for many years a member of the Communist Party" and also as "believing he could most effectively help to improve society through his research." It is not suggested that any of Burt's critics deliberately accused him of fraud, believing the charge to be false; only that their "passionate desires to get their own faiths confirmed" swayed their judgment, leading them to seize on every scrap of evidence, however implausible, to assault those who disagree with them.

It is remarkable that Hearnshaw never seems to have taken this possibility seriously, the more remarkable still since he rejected the claim that Burt himself was inspired by right-wing motives; and pointed out that, in so far as Burt had political preferences at all, they were liberal rather than conservative. Burt belonged to an earlier generation of progressive thinkers whose ideal was "equal opportunity." Heredity provided a rationale for the ideal, and mental testing a means of implementing it; so that, for them, equal opportunity was a happy combination of scientific fact and social value. The assumption that belief in heredity automatically entails right-wing views seems to be a relatively recent delusion, no more justified than the assumption that belief in environment necessitates left-wing sympathies. Of course, if Burt did not possess right-wing motives, he had other possible incentives to fraud, such as the desire to justify his life-long commitment to heredity. But it should not be forgotten that his critics had their motives too. However, the issue—scientific fraud or false accusation?—can only be decided, if it can be decided at all, by the evidence itself.

A Keen Nervousness

Scientists have a duty to be honest, like everyone else; and like everyone else, they are entitled to the presumption of innocence—the onus of proof lies with the accuser. But scientists also have a duty peculiar to themselves: to observe the regular technique of science. This is not a moral duty, but a professional obligation. If they fail, they are not wicked; they are incompetent. However eminent a scientist may be, the onus of proving competence still lies with him.

Burt published his account of his twin data in 1966 in an article in the *British Journal of Educational Psychology*, "The Evidence for the Concept of Intelligence." Much of the data had been collected many years before, during the 1920s and 1930s, in the course of his well-known survey of the abilities of London school children. The survey encountered many twins, and in the 1940s Burt extracted this material for special study and supplemented it with additional data. Several preliminary references to the twin data appeared before the final report of 1966. These occur in books and papers which were primarily concerned with more general questions; they are appended at points where evidence concerning heredity would be relevant; and they are brief—at most a couple of pages or so—omitting much of the information properly to be expected in experimental reports.

Burt left himself open to strong criticism for these anticipatory statements. He was expecting the reader to take his conclusions on trust, providing little or no information for critical assessment. He was treating clues as if they were evidence. Burt left himself open to the charge of arrogance, and it is not at all surprising to find J. Shields in his book *Monozygotic Twins: Brought Up Apart and Brought Up Together* commenting pointedly on the lack of detail in Burt's article, "Ability and Income," in *British Journal of Educational Psychology* in 1943. Burt's 1966 paper was a great improvement. It is not seriously deficient—at least by the standards of the time—with regard to the main types of information to be expected; though as with all such reports it is easy to find matters on which one would like more information. But is there in this whole series of publications, any evidence of deliberate fabrication? It should be borne in mind that the correlations Burt reported are very similar to those of other investigators, so there are no grounds for accusing him of attempting to deceive with respect to the strength of any hereditary effect. Kamin (1974) claimed that many of the correlations for intelligence Burt reported over the years had remained the same even though the number of subjects on which they were based had altered considerably. Such a finding is so unlikely as to be wholly unbelievable; and Kamin suggested that Burt had fabricated these correlations to give the impression of accuracy and reliability to his data on the inheritance of intelligence.

Undoubtedly many correlations remain the same in Burt's successive reports; indeed, there are even more than Kamin noticed. But Kamin seems to be mistaken in supposing that in all these cases the number of subjects had changed. The mistake arose largely because Burt did not always make clear, in his aforesaid inadequate preliminary reports, the number of subjects on which correlations were based. When these reports are compared with the 1966 report, it is easy to jump to conclusions that are, on more careful examination, found to be unjustified.

Burt reported three categories of correlation—for intelligence, for educational attainment, and for physique. The invariants are in fact found predominantly among the physical correlations, to a lesser extent among the educational, and least of all among those for intelligence. Kamin does not seem to have noticed this imbalance, though of the thirteen cases of invariance which he reports no less than eleven concerned physique or educational attainment; and of the two instances which concerned intelligence, one was corrected by Burt before he died, and the other may well have been a coincidence.

A possible explanation for the uneven distribution of the invariants would be that, as Burt gradually collected more data, there would come a time when he possessed as many measurements for physique and educational attainment as he needed to give reliable results, but when more measurements of the crucial intelligence levels were still advisable. In subsequent cases, the measurements for education and physique would then be dropped and attention concentrated on the assessment of intelligence.

Thus, when the final report was made public in 1966, the correlations for physique and educational attainment would be based on the smaller numbers collected at an earlier stage, and would therefore remain unchanged; whereas the correlations for intelligence would be based on larger numbers, and would therefore have altered. Something very like the observed distribution of repeated and new correlations would naturally result. Burt made clear both the 1955 and 1966 article that some of the correlations for physique were based on smaller numbers, but he did not explain why this was, nor did he give details of the precise numbers on which all the correlations were based on all occasions. Kamin seems to have been misled in part because he overlooked the distribution of the invariants, but also, and very excusably, by Burt's omission of sufficiently clear information about numbers.

But the omission of this information is a flimsy ground for accusing Burt of fabricating or manipulating his data. It is hard to see what Burt could have gained by the omission, because if anyone had wanted to know they could have asked him. The motive which Kamin ascribed to him is highly implausible. Correlations which remain constant even when numbers change are a statistical anomaly and suggest that something is wrong. The idea that Burt, an expert statistician, would concoct such results deliberately to demonstrate reliability, is absurd. He would know perfectly well that any such claim would be immediately rejected. The competent scientist produces a competent fabrication. Burt is certainly to be criticized for his omissions; but Kamin jumped to his conclusions altogether too quickly.

Another aspect was the case of the missing assistants. In 1976 Oliver Gillie, his suspicions aroused by reading Kamin, attempted to trace two female assistants with a view to questioning them about the kinship research. He contacted Tizard at the University of London Institute of Education who told him that he, Tizard, had already tried to find them, without success. Had Burt perhaps invented them? Gillie's search was equally unsuccessful, and in a *Sunday Times* article he promptly suggested that they may never have existed. Hearnshaw eventually added to these suspicions through his account of Burt's post-war diaries. These diaries, according to him, provided an extremely thorough and detailed account of Burt's activities, yet curiously failed to furnish any evidence that Burt had been in contact with his supposed assistants, or that they had been involved in collecting twin data, during this period. The absence of such evidence was in Hearnshaw's view decisive.

Burt recorded little information about the two assistants, and questions can certainly be asked to which Burt's papers contain no answer. As presented by Hearnshaw, the gaps in the record were made to seem very suspicious, especially in the context of Kamin's earlier doubts. But the "decisive evidence" of the diaries, as Hearnshaw called it, has proved to be nothing of the sort, as was shown by Ronald Fletcher as well as by Charlotte Banks and the present writer. They are far from being a complete or detailed record of Burt's activities.

Sometimes they are entirely empty for weeks and months on end; large stretches contain mainly domestic details, appointments, notes on the weather, and so on; detailed information about psychological matters is infrequent. The absence of reference to twins means virtually nothing. In any case, Burt himself said that most was collected earlier, before 1950, hence even if the diary record had been as complete as Hearnshaw alleges, twin references would probably be rare. In addition, the major gap—the missing assistants—has been remedied, at least to the extent of demonstrating that they really did exist.

Why, if most of Burt's data was collected before 1950, did he delay full publication until 1966? There are a number of possible explanations. He may have been collecting some additional cases (he was still appealing for more in 1955). He may have, as Banks suggests, been searching for some of his earlier data mislaid in wartime moves; competing pressures may have distracted him; increasing age and illness did not help. It is possible that he started inventing data in the 1950s or 1960s in order to present a stronger case for heredity. Hearnshaw accepts that Burt was working with authentic data up to and including 1955; but he thinks it possible that some at least of the additional cases reported subsequently were based on "reconstruction."

However, there is no positive evidence that Burt was doing this, and possibilities do not constitute evidence. There seems to be no strong reason for thinking that Burt could not have given a satisfactory answer to the questions that have been raised, if anyone had asked him. The onus of proof for fraud is on those who make the charge. There are many gaps in the record and Burt himself must take some responsibility for these, especially those in his preliminary reports. But omissions and misleading assertions are to be found among the critics, too, as was seen.

One of the most remarkable omissions concerns Jack Tizard and Alan and Ann Clarke. All played a prominent role in supporting the public attack on Burt's integrity in 1976, when Tizard was vice-president of the British Psychological Society, and Alan Clarke was president-elect; yet neither one provided a detailed account of their evidence, commensurate with the importance of the case. The Clarkes "worked mostly privately" as they state in 1980 in "Comments on Professor Hearnshaw's Balance Sheet on Burt," published in *A Balance Sheet on Burt, Supplement to the Bulletin of the British Psychological Society.*

When Eysenck asked for an inquiry in 1977, the Council of the British Psychological Society refused. When Hearnshaw in 1979 concluded that Burt was guilty, the Council accepted his conclusions forthwith, making no attempt to discover what might be said in Burt's defense. That Burt was unjustly treated has been recognized by writers as diverse as F. Samelson, who wrote in 1992 in an article, "Rescuing the Reputation of Sir Cyril Burt," in the *Journal of the History of the Behavioral Sciences*: "Joynson and Fletcher have a valid and important point to make when they raise the issue of the fairness of Burt's treatment." As Arthur Jensen remarked: "If ever there was a kangaroo court, this was it." The precise apportionment of praise and blame in the case of Cyril Burt may well have to be left to the day of judgment, when it will provide a severe test of the infallibility of the Almighty.

Meanwhile the significance of the affair lies in what it teaches us about the social sciences in general and psychology in particular. It reminds us that, even in the most advanced areas of experimental psychology, we do not possess objective methods which are wholly uninfluenced by fallible, personal judgment. In many other areas of psychology, especially in the applied field, the role of judgment may be even more extensive and still harder to control; and hence supposedly scientific conclusions may be profoundly affected by innumerable needs and interests, not least our political and social values.

12

Cyril Burt as the Victim of Scientific Hoax

J. Philippe Rushton

Cyril Burt's report of a preponderant genetic contribution to mental ability in monozygotic twins raised apart, flew in the face of two of this century's most powerful ideas: environmentalism and genetic equalitarianism. In 1961 Henry Garrett, a president of the American Psychological Association, referred to these as the "equalitarian dogma." In its strongest form, this dogma holds that all social groups—classes, races, and sexes—are genetically created equal in intellectual capacity and that disproportionate achievement was entirely the result of opportunity and other social factors.

Cyril Burt is featured in many psychology textbooks, not for his scientific discoveries, which were many, but for his alleged misrepresentation of data. By implication, the genetic basis of giftedness and intelligence is then held still not to be established. Meanwhile, new evidence from studies of twins raised apart have corroborated Burt's high heritability estimate, as have independent data from adoption and other family studies. Examination of the relationship of brain size to intelligence, and of race, sex, and social rank differences in brain size, suggest that Henry Garrett was correct to label the equalitarian dogma "the scientific hoax of the century." Cyril Burt was one of many victims of this hoax.

Denial of racial differences in IQ seems to have been what mostly fuelled the attack on Burt's integrity. Burt was concerned with differences of social class and only rarely strayed into discussion of race or gender differences. He held that the British upper classes contained a larger proportion of high genetic intelligence than did the British lower classes, even though, in absolute numbers, there would be more gifted

163

children outside of the upper classes than inside of them. (Child prodigies of humble origin were of special interest to him.) Because of his belief in the degree of overlap in the distributions, and also because of his belief that entrance into advanced school systems should be based on test and examination performance rather than the privilege of birth, Burt was considered a liberal in his day.

Burt's "day" was the 1920s and 1930s. He was born in 1883, the son of a medical doctor, and entered Oxford University in 1902 to read classics. While there he became enamored with the psychology of mental ability, a passion that was to last throughout his long life. He was a student of William McDougall, the instinct theorist and helped to collect data for Francis Galton, cousin to Charles Darwin. In 1913, Burt became an educational psychologist for London County Council. In 1924 he became professor of educational psychology, and in 1932 he succeeded to the chairmanship of the psychology department at University College. At this time he began to publish his studies showing a high heritability for IQ. In 1946 he was knighted by the Labour Government for his work on psychological testing and for making educational opportunities more widely available.

Burt broke new ground with the study of environmental effects, researching many family factors. In *The Backward Child*, published in 1937, he separated environmental variables of deprivation, such as poor nutrition and illness, from the innate factors that handicapped children. He advocated medical and dental examinations within the school setting to ensure that growth was proceeding normally and he was partly responsible for the daily distribution of milk to ensure adequate levels of vitamin D and the elimination of the scourge of rickets. In addition to malnutrition, he identified other physical causes of poor concentration such as defects of hearing, sight, speech, spinal curvature. He was one of the first to correlate sociological factors with poor school achievement, finding high relationships with residential indicators of infantile mortality, overcrowding, poverty, unemployment, family size, and the host of variables now only too familiar.

Burt was also interested in the factors affecting children at the top end of the scale. In *The Gifted Child*, published four years after his death, Burt focused on the damaging effects to a bright child, and to society, if the intelligence was not recognized because of the poverty of a child's background, inefficiency of the school system, or temperamental traits such as laziness in the child. Burt advocated special teaching and special classes, even special schools, for the gifted. He disapproved of the bias against the whole notion of giftedness manifested by equalitarianism.

Burt retired officially in 1950 but continued his scholarly activity. From 1947 to 1967 he was editor of the *British Journal of Statistical Psychology*. He also continued to publish data on the heritability of mental ability, including data from identical twins raised apart. These studies consistently suggested a large genetic contribution. Burt died in 1971 at the age of eighty-eight. His last book, *The Gifted Child*, was published posthumously in 1975.

The "Burt Affair" began in 1973 when Leon Kamin, then at Princeton University, claimed to have found discrepancies in some of Burt's figures, including an invariantly high correlation for IQ scores in twins raised apart. Despite the increase in sample size, from fifteen pairs in 1943 to fifty-three pairs in 1966, the correlation remained at a rounded 0.77. The scandal broke wide open with a story in the *Sunday Times* in 1976 headlined "Crucial Data Was Faked by Eminent Psychologist." The article charged not only that Burt had adjusted his data to suit his theory but that two of Burt's collaborators "may never have existed." The controversy flared for about three years. Then Burt's biographer Leslie Hearnshaw, a respected historian of psychology with access to Burt's private correspondence and diaries, concluded that Burt was "guilty." In 1980, the British Psychological Society, refusing to conduct an inquiry of its own, endorsed the guilty verdict. Even Burt's hereditarian defenders, Hans Eysenck in London and Arthur Jensen at Berkeley, withdrew their support.

The battle seemed over with an enormous victory for the equalitarians. Then, suddenly, in 1989, Robert B. Joynson re-opened the case and concluded that the accusations of fraud were ill-founded and that Burt must be exonerated. Working independently, Ronald Fletcher completed the demolition of the evidence for the prosecution, concluding with a "not proven." Fletcher drew out the implications, describing how ideology, in alliance with a receptive popular journalism and the media, established itself as a powerful third force in scientific discourse.

Many of the details of the case are fascinating and disturbing. For example, there is the truly "flabbergasting" fact (Jensen's term) that many of Burt's papers were destroyed by his housekeeper almost immediately after his death on the advice of Liam Hudson, professor of educational psychology at Edinburgh University, one of Burt's most ardent opponents. As Jensen has stated: "Both Hudson's rush to Burt's flat right after his death and his advice to Burt's secretary-housekeeper to burn the stored data seem stranger than fiction. Surely it must be one of the most bizarre events in the whole Burt affair."

On the most important issues, the matter appears settled. As for the so-called "missing" research assistants, they have been found. Of even greater importance, there have now been six studies of monozygotic twins raised apart. As Jensen, among others, has pointed out, Burt's data are by no means out of line with other findings. If an average is taken of the five other studies, weighted by sample size, the result is 0.75, almost the same as Burt's supposedly faked correlation of 0.77. Findings such as these led Sandra Scarr to title her 1986 presidential address to the Behavior Genetics Association "Three Cheers for Behavioral Genetics." She observed that "the war [between nature and nurture] is largely over." Scarr accepted that genetics underlay existing white social-class differences in IQ in the United States and Western Europe, although this may not have been the case for earlier generations when social mobility was more restricted. Large surveys have shown that a majority of experts believe that Scarr's opinion is correct and that the heritability of IQ in the American white population is about 60 percent, as reported by Mark Snyderman and Stanley Rothman.

The experts have been more cautious, however, in the matter of race. In her 1986 address, Scarr rejected a genetic explanation because racial barriers were less permeable than class barriers. She interpreted her own work as having shown an environmental cause for racial variation. I do not know whether she changed her opinion as a result of the recent debate, in the journal *Intelligence,* over her follow-up of black seventeen-year-olds raised by white, middle-class parents, in which the black, white, and mixed-race children's IQ scores are more accurately predicted by their biological origin than by the environment in which they were brought up.

It may seem strange that Burt should have been considered a liberal in his day. It will be salutory to remind ourselves of just how different the world of the 1970s (when Burt died) was from that of earlier decades. Internationally, the political spectrum had shifted to the far left. Over two-thirds of the world was ruled by communist or socialist dictatorships. Socialism seemed to be the wave of the future. Social class was no longer the issue.

With the demise of European imperialism and decolonization, the large influx of non-white immigrants into Europe, the American Civil Rights Movement, and the Vietnam War, race and gender became substitutes for social class in the rhetoric of exploitation, oppression, and liberation. Opposition to hierarchy generated the concept of "political correctness." Among the most politically incorrect scientific possibilities are evolution-based, genetic differences in brain size and intelligence between the races, the sexes, and the social classes. Yet, most recent data sets have shown clear evidence for exactly these group differences. Men's brains weigh an average of about 100 grams (8 percent) more than do women's brains, even after correction is made for the differences in body size, and Asians and Asian-Americans average proportionately larger brains than do Europeans and European-Americans who average larger than do Africans and African-Americans. Although group differences were widely believed to exist in the nineteenth and early twentieth century, more recently it has been thought that differences disappear when corrections are made for body size and other variables.

In a decisive recent study of sex differences in brain size, C. Davison Ankney reanalyzed well-controlled autopsy data from Cleveland, Ohio, in 1992. Based on 1,261 individuals between the ages of twenty-five and eighty, he found that, after correcting for body size, a 100-gram difference between men and women and between European-Americans and African-Americans. Men averaged 1328 grams and women 1223 grams; European-Americans averaged 1320 grams and African-Americans 1230 grams.

My own research confirmed Ankney's results in the use of a stratified random sample of 6,325 United States Army personnel measured in 1988 for fitting helmets and uniforms. After statistically adjusting for height, weight, rank, and then sex or race, I found that men averaged 110 cm^3 larger cranial capacities than women, and Asian-Americans averaged about 60 cm^3 larger than African-Americans, with European-Americans intermediate. In this study the sex difference was larger than the race difference. Men averaged 1442 cm^3 and women 1332 cm^3 and Asian-Americans, European-Americans, and African-Americans were, respectively, 1416, 1380, and 1359 cm^3. Military rank differences were also found. Officers averaged larger crania (1393 cm^3) than enlisted personnel (1375 cm^3), even after correcting for body size.

Subsequently, I examined world-wide data from the International Labour Office in Geneva. Head and body size figures were available from tens of thousands of men and women sampled from twenty different regions—East and West Africa, China and Japan, and European countries like Poland, France, Portugal, and Spain. After correcting for body size, cranial capacity for men averaged 160 cm^3 more than women, and Asians about 70 cm^3 more than Africans, with Europeans intermediate.

These studies do not stand alone. Since 1980 several analyses of group differences in brain size have been published, from autopsy and endocranial measures as well as from those based on external head perimeter. Historically, brain size data going back 100 years show Asians and Europeans with larger brains than Africans. A small, but robust, relation has been firmly established between mental ability and brain size. The correlation between test scores and brain size estimated from magnetic resonance imaging ranges from 0.35 to 0.47 with an average at about 0.40, as reported by Nancy Andreasen and colleagues in 1993 in the *American Journal of Psychiatry*. This represents a substantial increment over correlations reported since the turn of the century between head perimeter and measures of intelligence which average about 0.20.

Brain size-IQ relationships show up early in life. In the National Collaborative Perinatal Project, 19,000 black infants had smaller head perimeters at birth than 17,000 white infants, although black babies were also shorter in stature and lighter in weight. By age seven, catch-up growth favored the black children in body size but not in head perimeter. Head perimeter at birth correlated with IQ at age seven in both the black and the white children.

Group differences in brain size mediate differences in mental ability. With regard to gender differences in brain size, Ankney has pointed out a paradox. Women have smaller brains than men but apparently have the same intelligence test scores. Ankney resolved the problem by proposing that the sex difference in brain size relates to those intellectual abilities at which men excel. Men do better on various spatial tests and on tests of mathematical reasoning.

As for race differences, reviews of the global literature show that people of European ancestry living in North America, Europe, and Australia generally obtain mean IQs of around 100. People of East Asian ancestry living in North America and the Pacific Rim typically obtain slightly higher means, in the range of 101 to 111. Africans from south of the Sahara, African-Americans, and African-Caribbeans (including those living in Great Britain) obtain mean IQ scores between 70 and 90.

However, the vexing question of whether IQ test scores are at all revelatory about racial group differences in mental ability remains. At bottom, the problem hinges on whether the tests are culture-bound. Although a large body of technical work has disposed of this problem at the level of psychometric expertise —the tests show similar patterns of internal consistency and predictive validity for all groups, and the same differences are to be found on relatively culture-free tests—doubts linger in many quarters. Novel data on speed of decision making now show that the racial group differences in mental ability are pervasive. Cross-cultural investigations of reaction times have been carried out on nine-year-olds from five countries. In these tasks, subjects must decide which of several lights is on, or stands out from others, and move the hand to press a button. These responses take less than a second to make but brighter children make them significantly faster than less bright children. Richard Lynn found that oriental children from Hong Kong and Japan are faster in decision time than white children from Britain and Ireland, who in turn are faster than black children from Africa. Using the same tests on slightly older samples, Arthur Jensen has reported similar results in California.

These are not popular findings. They conflict with many deeply held values. Let me then emphasize the importance of not exaggerating the findings. There is enormous overlap in the distributions. The United States Army data showed only an 8 percent difference separating the men and women in cranial capacity and only a 4 percent difference separating Asian-Americans from African-Americans. Also, in the Army data, black officers averaged a larger cranial capacity (1369 cm^3) than white enlisted personnel (1366 cm^3). Clearly, it is highly problematic to generalize from a group average to any particular individual.

As a result of carrying this research on brain size, I, like Cyril Burt, had my reputation sullied. There was a call for my dismissal by the premier of Ontario, a criminal investigation by the Ontario Provincial Police, a media campaign against me, disruptions at the university, and an as yet unresolved investigation by the Ontario Human Rights Commission. Stories of harassment and intimidation could be told by others, among them Hans Eysenck in Great Britain, Arthur Jensen at Berkeley, Tom Bouchard at Minnesota, Richard Herrnstein at Harvard,

Linda Gottfredson at Delaware, and Michael Levin at City College of New York.

When Burt died in 1971, many people were gleeful. Equalitarian radicals were prepared to believe that Burt had committed fraud, long before any scandals were published. Charges of fraud were made all the time in personal conversation about the work then being published by Jensen and Eysenck. Charges of fraud are commonly raised in this research context. No one wanted to believe that there was a genetic basis to racial differences in intelligence.

It was the issue of race more than anything else that drove the attack on Burt. At that time, Burt's data was the lynchpin of Jensen's and Eysenck's work on race and it almost had to be discredited. Thus it was Leon Kamin in America who was the first serious critic of Burt and then, of course, many others entered the fray, including journalists and television producers.

Today, the campus radicals of earlier decades are the tenured radicals of the 1990s. Some are chairmen of departments, deans of faculties, and vice-presidents and presidents of universities. The 1960s mentality of peace, love, and above all equality now constitutes a significant portion of the intellectual establishment in the Western world. The equalitarian dogma is more, not less, entrenched than ever before. Yet, it is based on the scientific hoax of the century.

It is interesting that the hoax about genetic equality has been perpetuated for so long. Certainly one factor has been wishful thinking. We would all like the world to be different than in fact it is. Few have been eager to recognize the extent to which genes dictate what we are and what we may become. The power of genes, however, will become progressively harder to deny as the Human Genome Project nears completion. Many prefer not to know, because ignorance allows hope while knowledge can destroy it. The best way to predict your IQ is to average the IQ of your biological parents. That prediction holds regardless of whether you were raised totally separated from your biological parents. Ultimately we will be able to predict IQ scores by taking a single cell from an embryo.

For some, work on the genetics of intelligence, and racial differences therein, challenges the Enlightenment assumption that knowledge is always better than ignorance. But scholars have accepted that the earth is not the center of the universe, and that man's closest living relatives are the chimpanzees. We can yet affirm our common humanity by accepting our differences. The disparagement of Cyril Burt is the most extraordinary case of counterfeit charges in the history of academic psychology, if not all of science.

Recommended Readings

C. Davison Ankney. "Sex Differences in Relative Brain Size: The Mismeasure of Woman, Too?"*Intelligence* 16 (1992): 329–36.

Ronald Fletcher. *Science, Ideology, and the Media.* New Brunswick, N. J.: Transaction Publishers, 1991.

Arthur R. Jensen. "Scientific Fraud or False Accusations? The Case of Cyril Burt." In D. J. Miller and M. Hersen, eds., *Research Fraud in the Behavioral and Biomedical Sciences.* New York: John Wiley, 1992.

Richard Lynn. "Race Differences in Intelligence: A Global Perspective. *Mankind Quarterly* 31 (1991): 255–96.

Roger Pearson. *Race, Intelligence, and Bias in Academe.* Washington, D.C.: Scott-Townsend, 1991.

J. Philippe Rushton. "Cranial Capacity Related to Sex, Rank and Race in a Stratified Sample of 6,325 U.S. Military Personnel." *Intelligence* 16 (1992): 401–13.

Mark Snyderman and Stanley Rothman. *The IQ Controversy, the Media, and Public Policy.* New Brunswick, N. J.: Transaction Publishers, 1988.

13

Benevolent Misdiagnosis: Fraud by Euphemism in the Mental Health Professions

Nathaniel J. Pallone and James J. Hennessy

In the "learned professions," deception by impersonation (misrepresentation of one's credentials) has substantially receded in the face of ubiquitous state licensure procedures. Instead, deception is more likely to occur by misrepresentation of product; and the "product" at risk for misrepresentation is frequently the provision of a direct service on a fee-for-service basis rather directly amenable to audit procedures that are both formalized and external to the profession itself. Consider these contrasting situations:

- A psychologist in an academic setting, facing the ubiquitous need to publish or perish, fabricates data presumably reflecting a fictitious group of subjects, composes a manuscript that observes the usual canons governing scientific reporting (statistical tables, tests of significance, and the like), then packs it off to one of the 500 or so psychological and quasi-psychological journals that crowd the horizon. Because the manuscript claims no orgasmic, ground-breaking discoveries, it is given what will likely amount to only a cursory editorial board review in which the prospect of fabrication or falsification will surely not be paramount. In due course, the manuscript is published, the faculty member is promoted, and, unless there lurks a whistle-blower among his departmental colleagues, the world may never learn that deception has been perpetrated.
- A psychologist (or psychiatrist or social worker, for that matter) in private or hospital practice submits claim forms to a health insurance carrier on behalf of a patient, seeking payment for treatment sessions that are as fictitious as the subjects in his or her academic counterpart's fabricated study. Those claims forms are given a review that is not

173

cursory but rather detailed and may include direct contact with the patient for independent verification of the receipt of services. Should the fraud be uncovered, criminal charges are likely to be lodged not only against the practitioner but also against the patient who has at least tacitly consented to conspiracy. Moreover, should conviction result (even with suspended sentence), the practitioner will likely suffer additional sanctions (revocation or suspension of licensure) imposed by the governmental authority responsible for regulation of practice in his or her profession.

Few will fail to pronounce fraud in each case, although the intent, reward, target, and sanctions associated with each of the two pieces of fraudulent behavior may seem to vary inordinately. In the first case, we presume that the offender is motivated by ambition for academic promotion and that the benefit he or she hopes to realize is similarly represented by advancement in rank, with whatever increments in status and prestige may accrue. Should the fraud be detected, via whistle blowing or otherwise, the negative sanctions that will follow may include some form of public humiliation (in the wake of dismissal, for example). However, as sociologist Nachman Ben-Yehuda observes in one of the few extant empirical analyses of scientific fraud among behavioral scientists (which, rather tellingly, he elected to publish initially in the *British Journal of Criminology*), faculty members dismissed for fraudulent conduct rarely suffer more than momentary disruption in their careers, customarily garnering parallel academic appointments with only modest difficulty. In the second case, it is presumably naked avarice that has triggered the fraudulent behavior. But the probability of detection is greater by some order of magnitude, and we can rather confidently predict—especially in a period highly sensitized to spiraling health care costs—that, should its own audit procedures yield evidence of "probable cause," the health insurance carrier will press for punitive sanction, whether through the criminal courts, the licensing authority that regulates professional practice, or both.

Superficial observation might judge such differential sanctions appropriate. In the second case, after all, there is an identifiable aggrieved party that, however bureaucratic and impersonal an insurance company (or the federal or state government, through Medicare and Medicaid programs) may be, still seems more tangible than the abstract "world of truth" or "science of psychology." And, of course, in the second case, there is an actual cash value implicated in the fraudulent behavior, as if the garnering of a promotion in faculty rank accompanied by a salary increase does not also represent a ponderable "thing of value." In fact it may well outweigh by several hundred-fold all but the most egregious of comprehensively organized insurance fraud schemes. And there are indeed such schemes. In perhaps the most notorious case yet to come to light, Federal charges were leveled in the summer of 1993 against the nation's largest provider of private mental health services for fraudulent insurance claims in its several facilities amounting to a whopping $750 million.

Fraud by Benevolent Euphemism

As we observed in the introductory paper in this volume, charges of misconduct in professional psychology typically focus on sexual liaisons between therapists or counselors and their clients, while charges of fraud typically concern billing practices. Yet scant attention has been paid either in the scientific or professional literature to a widespread practice in the psychological professions (including not only psychology but also psychiatry, clinical social work, marriage and family counseling, substance abuse rehabilitation, and their several variants) far more frequent, namely, fraud by benevolent misdiagnosis. Consider this situation:

> A senior executive officer in a mid-size corporation, perceived as a "family man," suffers the penchant for sexual attraction to under-age girls. This unfortunate predilection leads to an encounter with the law; the humiliation of a public prosecution is avoided when the executive, who is well insured for mental health services (and who, for that matter, may also enjoy the benefits of "judicare" insurance), agrees to undergo professional mental health treatment. Accordingly, he avails himself of the services of a competent, but pricey, private mental health practitioner.

To insure that these services qualify for payment under the patient's health insurance plan, the practitioner must specify on the insurance claim form a diagnosis from the American Psychiatric Association's official lexicon, the *Diagnostic and Statistical Manual of Mental and Emotional Disorders*. Quite clearly, the appropriate diagnosis is some close approximation (represented by a five-digit numerical code) to "focused pedophilia, opposite sex, non-exclusive."

But, when he is handed the completed claim form by his therapist, our executive blanches in horror; the claim form must flow from his hand to that of a benefits clerk in the personnel department of the corporation of which he is an officer, thence to the insurance carrier. Oaths of confidentiality notwithstanding, our man fears that the state of his mental health will soon be bruited about the company cafeteria, amid muffled sniggers. "Doc, don't you think—" he importunes. And, a few steps down the line, a revised claim form is produced, which bears the rather benign diagnosis "adjustment reaction of adulthood." There may ensue some speculation in the cafeteria, but few sniggers.

Little question arises as to whether fraud has been committed, at least in the technical sense of the receipt of something of value on the basis of misrepresentation. But there is not the slightest evidence of malicious intent. Instead, the practitioner will confidently argue that he or she has displayed the most delicate sensitivity toward the patient and that, in so doing, he or she has not only protected what remains of the patient's sense of dignity (the destruction of which, he or she will assert, would incalculably impede the therapeutic process), while also and not incidentally preserving the patient's value to his corporation, the economic welfare of which is what provides employment to the prospective sniggerers in the company cafeteria. Moreover, since the services have indeed been rendered and since the insurance carrier is obligated to the same level of payment whatever the diagnosis, no aggrieved party is readily identifiable. To the extent that an intent to harm is implicated in pronouncing a behavior as criminal, it is difficult to discern in this situation. Far from harming the patient, the practitioner's motivation is clearly to protect.

Most people would consider it a harmless "white lie" at worst, or (in a strangely color-contrasted metaphor) a "gray area"—clearly analogous to the situation in which the plastic surgeon "finds a way" (the term universally employed in the professions to denominate benevolent misdiagnosis) to convincingly call cosmetic (and therefore elective) surgery "reconstructive" and thus medically necessary. Maverick psychiatrist Thomas Szasz would doubtless decry the defining of patently criminal behavior as pathological.

Down the pike, of course, there may lurk consequent problems. By its very definition, the diagnostic condition known as "adjustment reaction" is relatively transitory. Should our executive's condition prove rather more intractable, and require extended therapy, the insurance carrier may balk at payment for long-term treatment for a transitory disorder. If we wish to spin out the tale into horror show dimensions, we might consider that the competent mental health professional might wish to employ as an adjunct to verbal psychotherapeutic treatment the powerful anti-psychotic medication fluoxetine hydrochloride (Prozac), which has, in recent studies at Boston's McLean Hospital, shown remarkable results in controlling the behavior (though not the appetites or fantasies) of focused pedophiles. Now the pharmacist who fills the prescription enters the act, along with the physician who writes it, if the primary therapist is not a psychiatrist; either they too enter the benevolent collusion or they incline to join the sniggering. In the most extreme scenario, a pharmacist mindful of the ethical canons of the profession of pharmacy, no less than of federal and state regulations governing the dispensing of psychotropic medication, may simply refuse to fill a prescription for a drug that is contra-indicated for a benign and transient condition. One cannot reasonably predicate a willingness to disregard the canons governing the ethical practice of medicine to all those who are empowered to write prescriptions, so that he or she may record a dead-accurate diagnosis on the claim form filed on behalf of the patient with the same insurance carrier. If the scenario unfolds in that direction, the insurance carrier is now faced either with data that cannot be interpreted in any meaningful way or with presumptive evidence of collusion.

In actual practice, when a demurrer to payment for prolonged treatment of a relatively benign and short-lived disorder is fielded by a third-party payer, the inventive clinician and the patient merely collude to provide yet another euphemistically, but benevolently, inaccurate diagnosis—perhaps even colluding to suggest that the "new" disorder has arisen sequentially to, and independently of, the initial condition to which a euphemistically inaccurate diagnosis was benevolently applied.

Political Correctness and Psychiatric Nosology: Boomerang Effect

One suspects that benevolent misdiagnosis became a feature of the conceptual landscape in the mental health professions when (as the result of massive lobbying efforts on the part of organizations representing mental health care providers) the costs of mental health care began to shift from the patient to health insurance carriers. But the practice became visibly prevalent in the mid-1970s, as the unintended and unforeseen consequence of an act of benevolence on the part of the American Psychiatric Association, the sole arbiter in this country of what is and is not a mental or emotional disorder.

Bowing to an early version of what has come to be called political correctness, the American Psychiatric Association temporarily (as later events proved) excluded homosexuality from its lexicon of mental and emotional disorders—a decision that yielded the unanticipated consequence of stranding homosexual men and women then actively involved in psychotherapeutic treatment paid for by their insurance carriers. Why, those carriers reasoned quite logically, should we continue to pay for your mental health treatment when the "disorder" for which you are being treated no longer officially exists?

Consistent with the views of Freud and Krafft-Ebbing, not to mention with the strictures of most Western religions, the definition of sexual deviation in the first (1952) edition of the American Psychiatric Association's *Diagnostic and Statistical Manual* was unforgiving in categorizing homosexuality in any form as a mental illness, and indeed the criminal codes of the various states contemporaneously proscribed such behavior. But, two decades later in the exemplar *par excellence* of the politics of psychiatric nosology, homosexuality temporarily vanished from the official lexicon of mental disorders. It was replaced in the third edition with "ego-dystonic homosexuality," in which the emphasis was placed on anxiety and depression resultant from gender preference (and typically arising from the reactions of others rather than from within the individual, that is, *extra*psychically and *inter*personally, not intrapsychically and intrapersonally). In 1994, the fourth edition of the *Manual* made its long-heralded appearance, and, wonder of wonders, the relatively simple diagnosis of homosexuality reappeared, but with the verbosely euphemistic title "gender identity disorder in adolescents or adults—sexually attracted to males," or as the case may be, "sexually attracted to females," with "sexually attracted to both" and "sexually attracted to neither" thrown in, one presumes, to satisfy "equal time" considerations.

The definitive social history of the political dynamics that led ↑ ⊃ the mid-1970s decision of the American Psychiatric Association to e⅄ :lude homosexuality from the second edition of its official lexicⁿ ⸳ of ⸳ental illnesses is yet to be written, though accounts in the popu˙ɑr p ⸳ss were voluble. In his *Insanity: The Idea and Its Consequences,* Tho⍨⸳as Szasz attributes the decision to "pressure from gay rights groups." Certainly the efforts of organizations representing the interests of gay men and women, then initiating pioneering struggles against discrimination on the basis of what has come to be called "gender preference," were potent. But it is likely that that decision also represented a sort of backlash against conceptual formulations of mental health and illness rooted in orthodox Freudian psychoanalytic theory.

Best expressed in Freud's *Three Essays on the Theory of Sexuality* (originally published in 1905), psychoanalytic theory had long held that homosexuality, whether among men or among women, represents an arresting of psychosexual development at a pre-adult level and that only heterosexuality is consistent with adult psychosexual functioning, so that even consensual homosexuality between (or even among) adults is to be regarded as the manifestation of psychopathological disorder. As the prestigious Group for the Advancement of Psychiatry (associated with the Menninger Clinic) put it in a remarkable 1955 document entitled *Report on Homosexuality with Particular Emphasis on This Problem in Governmental Agencies,* phrased in categorically unforgiving psychoanalytic terms: "Homosexuality is an arrest at, or a regression to, an immature level of psychosexual development." Perhaps there lurked lingering resentment among the more scientifically oriented members of the psychiatric community about the over-reliance of the APA's earlier editions of the *Diagnostic and Statistical Manual* (1952, 1968) on psychoanalytic formulations of mental health and illness generally. The resentment may be due to the fact that the earlier editions are grounded in elaborate and intellectually satisfying conceptualizations with little empirical support, which thus seem to many to constitute artistic rather than scientific creations.

But, at least among practicing clinicians, the midway reversal in adding *ego-dystonic homosexuality* to the third edition and the euphemistic recrudescence of the unalloyed disorder in the fourth edition of the American Psychiatric Association lexicon are understood as functions of the *economics* of mental health care. So long as a particular individual seeks professional treatment for a recognized mental disorder (i.e., one enumerated in the APA's official lexicon), his or her health insurance carrier has little choice but to provide payment; removal of homosexuality in any form from the lexicon had the effect of permitting those carriers to deny claims for treatment when the focal behavior denotes a diagnostic category that had been summarily eliminated from the official lexicon.

There is no published record of the discussions between the champions of gay rights who lobbied the APA prior to its mid-1970s decision and those targets of their benevolence stranded by that decision. But it is unquestioned that inventive, protective clinicians "found a way" to substitute a benevolent misdiagnosis so as not to trammel the progress of treatment.

Frequently, that diagnosis was listed on the insurance claim form as "adjustment reaction with depressed mood." What the patients so affected were adjusting to, of course, was the economic impact of the benevolence of their champions; and what they were depressed about was their quite predictable abandonment by their insurance carriers. Not incidentally, were one to have taken a mental health census of the nation during those years of ignorance of the impact of political correctness on formal psychiatric nosology, one would have been struck by the sudden disappearance of homosexuality as a mental health problem and the rapidity with which "adjustment reaction" reached epidemic proportions.

Trend spotters, beware the temptation: May it be that it is relatively easier to alter psychological diagnoses or to interchange vague and nonspecific "disorders" like "gender preference" and "adjustment reaction" than it is to claim that an infected appendix has been surgically removed when radiologic examination will reveal that the appendix is precisely where it ought to be, and in quite a healthy state?

Misdiagnosis and Mental Health Planning

Quite apart from whether the practice of benevolent misdiagnosis in the mental health professions merely conforms to the equally widespread parallel custom in medicine and dentistry, we can with some confidence multiply our pedophilic senior executive by hundreds of thousands of cases per year. We might now factor in the research of investigators like Lewis Goldberg or Robyn Dawes on the prevalence of inaccuracy in psycho-diagnosis. In some studies, it has been reported that the prevalence of misdiagnosis (not necessarily conscious, deliberate, or benevolent) hovers near 75 percent in the caseloads of even highly experienced mental health clinicians. Unless we are willing to accept an explanation that veers in the direction of gross incompetence among members of the mental health professions, it would be foolhardy to discount consciously inaccurate diagnosis by benevolence and/or euphemism as a major contributing factor.

As a nation, we stand somewhere near a change of major or minor magnitude in the delivery of health care services. A soundly anchored public policy for the planning of programs and services in mental health and the charting of personnel needed to staff such programs and services would seem to require data of several sorts. First, we will need data such as are now gathered under auspices of the National Institutes of Mental Health through the periodic epidemiological studies of mental health and illness based on screening interviews of random, stratified samples of the population. Such data can be expected to yield solid indices of the relative incidence of mental disorders by diagnostic category. Second, we need data which indicate with some specificity those disorders for which persons with access to mental health services are willing to seek professional assistance; some persons might, for example, be more inclined to seek assistance from non-professional sources (self-help groups, family members, pastors, scout leaders, even bartenders) than from mental health clinicians, while others who acknowledge the need for assistance may nonetheless decline to seek or to accept help from either professional or non-professional sources. From these two sets of data, we should be able to extrapolate on a rational basis to personnel needs for both professional clinicians and non-professional sources of assistance.

Quite logically, we should expect an enumeration of the aggregate data already on hand in the records of the major health insurance carriers (and the federal Medicare and Medicaid programs) to provide essential information on the sorts of disorders for which treatment is actually sought by those who presently are able to avail themselves of professional treatment. But those data are fraught with inaccuracies, conscious, euphemistic, benevolent, and otherwise. Societally, the price we pay for benevolent misdiagnosis may be that any approximation to such data cannot proceed on the basis of current records but must rest on sheer guesswork. The price the mental health professions pay is the fostering of a general perception that the process of mental health diagnosis is driven by the economics of health care rather than by a concern for scientific or quasi-scientific accuracy and that the clinician himself or herself differs little from the hired gun.

Recommended Readings

Nachman Ben-Yehuda. "Deviance in Science." *British Journal of Criminology* 26, no. 1 (1986): 1–27.

Robyn M. Dawes. *House of Cards: Psychology and Psychotherapy Built on Myth.* New York: Free Press, 1994.

Thomas Szasz. *Insanity: The Idea and Its Consequences.* New York: John Wiley, 1987.

Contributors

James S. Coleman was University Professor of Sociology at the University of Chicago and president of American Sociological Association.

Neil Gilbert is Chernin Professor of Social Welfare and Social Services at the University of California at Berkeley. He is the author of *Capitalism and the Welfare State* and *Clients and Constituents*.

David Goodstein is professor of physics and applied physics and vice provost at the California Institute of Technology and a frequent contributor to scholarly literature. He is the author of *States of Matter* and creator of the Public Broadcasting System's series "The Mechanical Universe." His paper originally appeared in the *American Scholar.*

Linda S. Gottfredson is professor of educational studies at the University of Delaware and co-director of the Project for the Study of Intelligence and Society.

James J. Hennessy is professor and chairman of the Division of Psychological Services in the Graduate School of Education at Fordham University, New York. He is the coauthor (with Nathaniel J. Pallone) of *Criminal Behavior: A Process Psychology Analysis.*

Irving Louis Horowitz is Hannah Arendt Professor of Political Science and Sociology at Rutgers University. He is the author of *The Conscience of Worms and the Cowardice of Lions* and *Persuasions and Prejudices.*

Robert B. Joynson is the author of *The Burt Affair,* published by Routledge in 1989. He is a British psychologist who resides at Ormonde House. He was formerly with the Department of Psychology at the University of Nottingham.

Edith Kurzweil is distinguished university professor of sociology at Adelphi University and executive editor of *Partisan Review*. Her most recent book is *The Freudians: A Comparative Perspective.* She is working on a book titled *Freudians and Feminists: A Sociological Perspective.*

Marcel C. LaFollette is associate research professor of science and technology policy at the Center for International Science and Technology Policy at George Washington University, Washington, DC. She is the author of *Stealing into Print: Fraud, Plagiarism, and Other Misconduct in Scientific Publishing.*

Mary Lefkowitz is a classicist and Andrew W. Mellon Professor in the Humanities at Wellesley College. She is writing a book titled *Mythistory: The Deconstruction of Ancient Greece.*

Richard Ofshe is professor of sociology at the University of California at Berkeley. He shared in a 1979 Pulitzer prize for an exposé of Synanon and a 1994 Pulitzer Prize for "Making Monsters," which originally appeared in *Society* 30:3. His other books include *Interpersonal Behavior in Small Groups* and *Utility and Choice in Social Interaction.*

Nathaniel J. Pallone is University Distinguished Professor, psychology and criminal justice, at Rutgers—The State University of New Jersey. He is the author of *Mental Disorder among Prisoners* and coauthor (with James J. Hennessy) of *Criminal Behavior: A Process Psychology Analysis,* both published by Transaction.

J. Philippe Rushton is professor of psychology at the University of Western Ontario, Canada. He is the author of *Race, Evolution, and Behavior,* published by Transaction, and *Altruism, Socialization, and Society.*

Del Thiessen is professor of psychology at the University of Texas in Austin. His research is focused on human evolution and mate selection. He is the author or coauthor of five books and a wide number of research publications.

Ethan Watters is a freelance journalist who has written on Satanic panic and the false memory phenomenon.

Robert K. Young is professor of psychology at the University of Texas in Austin. His research is focused on human memory and individual differences. He has published widely on statistical techniques and experimental design and is currently teaching in these areas.

Index